P<!---->Sun<!---->school<!---->Ne<!---->ry

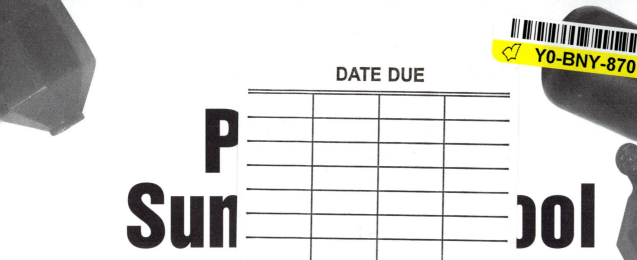
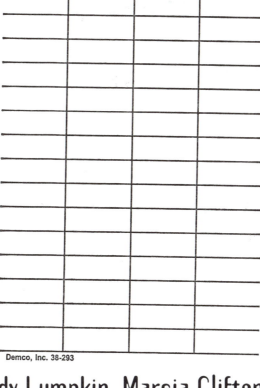

Cindy Lumpkin, Marcia Clifton,
Yevonne Donkervoet, Cindy Morris,
Paula Stringer, and R. Scott Wiley
and Thomas Sanders

LIFEWAY PRESS
NASHVILLE, TENNESSEE

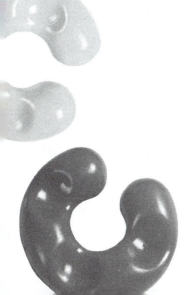

© Copyright 1999 LifeWay Press
All rights reserved

No part of this work may be reproduced or transmitted in any form or by any means, electronic or mechanical, including photocopying and recording, or by any information storage or retrieval system, except as may be expressly permitted in writing by the publisher. Requests for permission should be addressed in writing to LifeWay Press, 127 Ninth Avenue North, Nashville, Tennessee 37234-0173.

ISBN 0-7673-9986-2

This book is a resource in the Leadership and Skill Development category of the Christian Growth Study Plan and is used to fill the requirements of courses numbered LS-0013 and LS-0068.

Dewey Decimal Classification Number: 268.432
Subject Heading: SUNDAY SCHOOL—CHILDREN

Printed in the United States of America

Sunday School Group
LifeWay Church Resources, a division of
LifeWay Christian Resources of the Southern Baptist Convention
127 Ninth Avenue North Nashville, Tennessee 37234

Unless otherwise noted, all Scripture passages printed herein are from the Holy Bible,
New International Version
© copyright 1973, 1978, 1984
by International Bible Society.
Used by permission.

Table of CONTENTS

Meet the Authors............................4

Foreward...................................5

Connecting with the Future 6

Connecting with Preschoolers 12

Connecting Through Planning................22

Connecting with Leadership..................36

Connecting Through Ministry 46

Connecting Through Teaching 56

Appendix
    Preschool Resource Management..............70
    Room Arrangements........................73

    Studying This Book........................77
        Church Growth Study Plan..................80

Meet the AUTHORS

Marcia Clifton teaches preschoolers at Eastwood Baptist Church in Owasso, Oklahoma.

Yevonne Donkervoet serves as preschool minister at Fielder Road Baptist Church in Arlington, Texas.

Cindy Lumpkin teaches preschoolers at Forest Hills Baptist Church in Franklin, Tennessee. She is manager of the Preschool Ministry Services Section, LifeWay Christian Resources.

Cindy Morris serves as preschool associate for the Sunday School Department of the South Carolina Baptist Convention, Columbia, South Carolina.

Thomas Sanders teaches preschoolers at First Baptist Church, Goodlettsville, Tennessee. He is director of the Preschool Sunday School Ministry Department, LifeWay Christian Resources.

Paula Stringer is professor of childhood education at New Orleans Baptist Theological Seminary, New Orleans, Louisiana.

R. Scott Wiley is a preschool teacher at Tulip Grove Baptist Church in Hermitage, Tennessee, and multimedia designer in the Preschool Ministry Services Section, LifeWay Christian Resources.

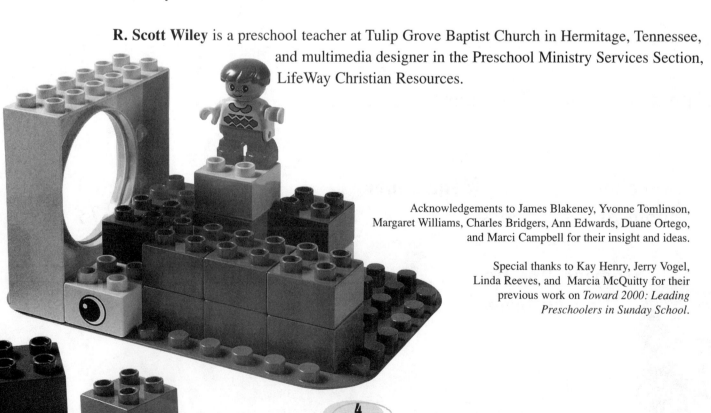

Acknowledgements to James Blakeney, Yvonne Tomlinson, Margaret Williams, Charles Bridgers, Ann Edwards, Duane Ortego, and Marci Campbell for their insight and ideas.

Special thanks to Kay Henry, Jerry Vogel, Linda Reeves, and Marcia McQuitty for their previous work on *Toward 2000: Leading Preschoolers in Sunday School*.

FOREWORD
by Bill Taylor

It was time. The world God had created had chosen its own way and was hopelessly lost. He had a strategy that would transform the world—one that would replace fear with faith, despair with hope, hatred with love, spiritual darkness with light.

God chose to enter the kingdom of this world personally, in Jesus Christ, transforming forever anyone who would receive Him. The kingdom of this world was intersected, once and for all, by the kingdom of God. Through Jesus, God overcame sin and death with His righteousness and eternal life.

Jesus demonstrated God's love for all people. His life and ministry were a living portrait of perfect love. Jesus loved God with His entire heart, soul, mind, and strength; and He loved His neighbor as He did Himself. Jesus demonstrated this love by obediently fulfilling God's strategy to reconcile a lost world to Himself. Jesus willingly submitted His life as a sacrifice, through death on a cross, to free each of us from the ultimate penalty for our sin. Jesus made a way for us to receive abundant, eternal life. Everything about Jesus revealed God's strategy to act.

Jesus' mission extends to all of His disciples throughout time. He has called us to continue His work, and He has equipped us for that work (Matt. 28:18-20). We are to be transformed people. We are to be agents of transformation.

God has given us a powerful and underutilized tool in that transforming task. Sunday School is the strategy that can engage people in Great Commission ministry, leading them to faith in the Lord Jesus Christ and building Great Commission Christians. When people gather to encounter God through the study of His Word in the company of His people, the Lord is with them in a special way. Sunday School must stay firmly grounded in God's living and written Word. However, there is more to Sunday School for a new century than gathering for Bible study, as important as that is.

In the 21st century, Sunday School must provide opportunities for people to come to know Christ and to engage Christians in leading others to faith in Him. Sunday School for a new century must provide seven-day-a-week opportunities to grow in understanding of and in obedience to God's Word. It must provide opportunities for people to express their love for God and for people by engaging them in ministry and missions. Sunday School must build unity and fellowship in the church, and help people find ways to express their love for God in all that they do.

It is time. It is time because of the opportunities. Today churches have a wonderful opportunity to fulfill the Lord's command. The new world of the 21st century and the third millennium is not unlike the world God entered when He divided time forever with Jesus' birth. Our world, continuing to choose its own way, remains hopelessly lost without Christ. It is time because of this overwhelming need.

Your time is now.

CHAPTER 1
Connecting with

The Future Begins Today

Maria hesitantly cleared her throat.

"Pastor," she said, "I'd like to talk to you about the preschool class. When I dropped off my children on Sunday, I noticed someone different was helping Mrs. Brenda."

Pastor Mike nodded. "Yes. Now that we have 10 preschoolers, we're trying to find another teacher for that class. I hope you will be patient with us."

"I'm not here to complain," Maria said quickly. "I am just concerned that we are not doing enough to help our preschoolers grow in their understanding of God. I've been thinking and praying, and I feel that I would like to volunteer."

***

"Will you serve as our Preschool Division director?" asked Rose.

"Why do we need a division director?" Kent asked.

"Our church is growing, and we sense the need to organize our preschool departments into a division. This way, we can minister more effectively to the young families in our community," Rose explained.

"OK," Kent said, "but why me?"

"Kent, you have such a passion for teaching preschoolers and ministering to their families. Since you made the commitment to teach, you have continued to learn about preschoolers. We need someone with your training and passion to help lead other teachers and directors."

"Passion? I never thought of it that way. You know, when I first started teaching, it was just to help out. But the more I was around preschoolers, I began to understand the importance of laying spiritual foundations in their lives. Two weeks ago, when 14-year-old Justin made a profession of faith, I realized that I had helped introduce him to God's love when he was in my preschool department." Kent paused. "I will think and pray about where God can use me."

Making the Connection

What situations in our society threaten the opportunity for spiritual transformation in your life, in your family, and in your church?

What changes and commitments will you and your church need to make in order to see spiritual transformation?

THE GREAT COMMISSION
"Go and make disciples of all nations, baptizing them in the name of the Father and of the Son and of the Holy Spirit, and teaching them to obey everything I have commanded you. And surely I am with you always, to the very end of the age."
(Matthew 28:19-20)

The Future

Change is inevitable. A 101-year-old lady was asked, "What is the most significant change you have seen in your lifetime?" She replied, "How I travel." During her lifetime she has traveled by buggy, car, train, and plane. She continued by saying that change could be good or bad, depending on how it is used. Change is good when used to make the world a better place and help people know about God. Each day of her life, she had the choice of allowing change to stop her or help her move forward. What kept her on the right path amid all the changes? It was the values learned from her parents and her willingness to accept changes that did not jeopardize those values.

As we face the close of a century full of change and embrace a new millennium of opportunity, we are challenged to consider the impact that culture, society, and church will make on young families.

Through all of these changes, we must attempt to keep our balance and stay in tune with God. As we look at teaching preschoolers the powerful truths of the Bible, we must keep God's perspective—a kingdom perspective—as we move toward a spiritual transformation in our lives and the lives we touch. We must evaluate our traditions and decide what we need to carry forward into the future and what we must change in order to meet the needs of young families.

We have a biblical mandate to partner with parents and teach children. No other Scripture passage more clearly instructs teachers and parents to guide their children to God than Deuteronomy 6:5-7: "Love the Lord your God with all your heart and with all your soul and with all your strength. These commandments that I give you today are to be upon your hearts. Impress them on your children. Talk about them when you sit at home and when you walk along the road, when you lie down and when you get up." The task is clear—to teach children in all walks of life.

Teaching preschoolers about God is a biblical mandate.

Connecting with the Future

Preschool teachers partner with parents in guiding preschoolers toward an understanding of God, Jesus, the Bible, church, self, others, family, and God's creation. As preschoolers come to church for Sunday School, Discipleship Training, Mission Friends, weekday education, or preschool music, they need teachers who understand them and how they learn. All teachers must be consistent, teaching preschoolers the same foundational concepts with the same methods.

What is Sunday School?

Sunday School is the foundational strategy in a local church for leading people to faith in the Lord Jesus Christ and for building Great Commission Christians through Bible study groups that engage people in evangelism, discipleship, fellowship, ministry, and worship.

The Great Commission is the driving force behind all that occurs in Sunday School and other Bible-teaching opportunities during the week. The church should have a balance among five essential functions—evangelism, discipleship, ministry, fellowship, and worship.

What is Sunday School to preschool teachers, preschoolers, and their families? Sunday School is the foundational strategy that introduces preschoolers to God and begins the process toward conversion and spiritual transformation. Through Sunday School, teachers can share their faith with parents of preschoolers, minister to preschoolers and their families, offer times of fellowship, and lead preschoolers to develop an understanding of worship through the use of Bible stories, songs, Bible phrases and verses, and prayer.

Making the Connection

Use the following letters to describe what preschool Sunday School means to you.

S — Study your Bible
U
N
D
A
Y

S
C
H — Heart
O
O
L

Principles for the 21st Century Sunday School

"Kent," said Rose, "as you consider becoming division director, I want you to understand how the preschool ministry is an important part of our church's Sunday School strategy. I want to share with you the principles of Sunday School."

The Principle of Foundational Evangelism:
Sunday School is the foundational evangelism strategy of the church.
1. Sunday School emphasizes ongoing, open Bible study groups that reproduce new groups as the best long-term approach for building a ministry environment that guides preschoolers and children toward conversion through foundational teaching, encourages unsaved people to come to faith in Christ, assimilates new believers into the life of the church, and encourages believers to lead others to Christ.
2. Sunday School provides the most efficient churchwide evangelism training network to equip members to become passionate soul-winners.
3. Sunday School encourages Bible study in short-term groups and through special Bible teaching events as effective ways to promote outreach and evangelism and to address specific life concerns, spiritual issues, church functions, and doctrinal issues.
4. Sunday School creates a great center for missionary power as people tell and live the wondrous story of Christ's redeeming love.

The Principle of Foundational Discipleship:
Knowing God through Jesus is the first step of discipleship. Sunday School is the seven-day-a-week strategy and Bible study is a foundational step of discipleship for involving people in seeking the Kingdom of God and fulfilling the Great Commission.
1. Sunday School provides the primary organizational framework for involving families and individuals in the comprehensive work of the church including evangelism, discipleship, ministry, fellowship, and worship.
2. Sunday School provides foundational discipleship and encourages members to strengthen their Christian walk by participating in other discipleship opportunities.
3. Sunday School emphasizes that every member who is a believer must become accountable for the responsibility God has given him or her as a minister and missionary to the world.
4. Sunday School supports all other church ministries and intentionally encourages its members to be good stewards, fully involved in the church's overall mission.

The Principle of Family Responsibility:
Sunday School affirms the home as the center of biblical guidance.

1. Sunday School helps equip Christian parents, including single parents, to fulfill their responsibility as the primary Bible teachers and disciplers of their children.
2. Sunday School encourages Christian parents who by word and deed guide their children to integrate the Scriptures into their lives, influencing how they think and act.
3. Sunday School involves families in the comprehensive work of the church.
4. Sunday School works to nurture sound and healthy families and seeks to lead non-Christian parents to Christ.

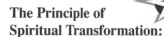

The Principle of Spiritual Transformation:
Sunday School engages learners in the biblical model of instruction that leads to spiritual transformation.
1. Sunday School affirms that spiritual transformation is God's work of changing a believer into the likeness of Jesus by creating a new identity in Christ and by empowering a lifelong relationship of love, trust, and obedience to glorify God.
2. Sunday School champions the absolute truth and authority of the Word of God and compels believers to integrate a biblical worldview into their minds, hearts, and lives through ongoing, systematic Bible study.
3. Sunday School recognizes that Bible study is most effective when it occurs in the context of the learner's total life, especially family relationships, and when it considers the special needs, generational perspective, age and life-stage characteristics and learning styles of the learner.
4. Sunday School addresses transcultural life issues common to individuals, churches, families, tribes, and nations regardless of geographic, ethnic, or language identity.

The Principle of Biblical Leadership:
Sunday School calls leaders to follow the biblical standard of leadership.

1. Sunday School affirms the pastor as the primary leader in its ministry of building Great Commission Christians.
2. Sunday School calls leaders to a prophetic ministry, listening to God's voice, discerning His message, integrating the message into their lives, and proclaiming His truth through His church to nations.
3. Sunday School recognizes that the leader is the lesson in that every leader is accountable for being an authentic example of Christianity in personal living and producing new leaders for service through the ministries of the church.
4. Sunday School recognizes that planning is essential to implementing its strategy.

Throughout this book you will see strategic principle icons to show how these principles relate to Preschool Sunday School. Although the when, where, and how of Preschool Sunday School may have changed over the years, some underlying preschool principles remain true. Each of these preschool principles strengthens and undergirds the overall principles of Sunday School.

Principle of Foundational Evangelism:
- Preschool teachers witness to unsaved parents and guide them to become involved in the total life of the church.
- Preschool teachers build foundations in the lives of preschoolers that form a base for conversion later in life.

Principle of Foundational Discipleship:
- Preschool teachers help preschoolers discover basic concepts regarding God, Jesus, the Bible, church, others, self, family, and God's creation.
- Preschoolers begin to develop understanding about how they are to live and relate to others and how God and the church can be important in their lives.

Principle of Family Responsibility:
- Parents and teachers work together in spiritual education, understanding that parents are the primary spiritual teachers in preschoolers' lives.

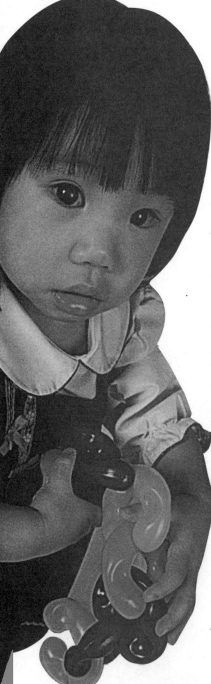

- The Preschool Division can provide tools and resources for parents to use in teaching preschoolers the Bible at home.
- Preschool leaders can mentor parents.

Principle of Spiritual Transformation:
- Preschool Sunday School builds foundations that lead to spiritual transformation later in life.
- Preschool curriculum is Bible-based and child-centered.
- Preschool teachers lead preschoolers in Bible-learning experiences that are experiential, active, involving, and suitable for the age. Teachers consider age, needs, development, and level of learning of the preschoolers as they plan Bible-learning centers/activities.
- Preschool teachers encourage preschoolers to make choices so that they can learn in the ways that God has gifted them to learn.
- Preschool rooms have space, equipment, and resources that invite preschoolers to make choices and move safely among Bible-learning centers/activities.

Principle of Biblical Leadership:
- Preschool teachers recognize that preschoolers learn through example, so teachers live as examples of followers of Christ.
- Preschool teachers provide consistency in attendance, schedule, and room environment each week. Regular planning helps maintain consistency.
- Preschool classes/departments maintain proper teacher/child ratios to ensure positive interaction and warm relationships.
- Preschool teachers are involved in planning, training, and other activities that maximize the teaching session and develop them as leaders.

> Kent approached Rose, "I have prayed and decided that I will be the division director next year. Should I contact the leaders of other preschool programs and talk about how we can all work together?"
>
> Rose replied, "Good thinking. Sunday School is just one area of ministry in our church. As our church grows, we will need to work even harder to make sure that each ministry works together to provide the best teaching and learning environment for our preschoolers."

Sunday School is the foundation of preschool ministry, but it does not function alone.

Sunday School is the foundation of preschool ministry, but it does not function alone. In a well-rounded ministry, Sunday School, Discipleship Training, preschool music, missions education, and Church Weekday Education must work hand in hand to provide consistent, effective teaching for preschoolers. Each area of preschool ministry should be a part of establishing and upholding policies that provide a safe and secure environment for preschoolers. The teachers in each area need to agree on consistent teaching methods. Whatever the size of the church, training and communication are keys to a successful preschool ministry.

Understanding how preschool Sunday School relates to the overarching principles of Sunday School is just the beginning of organizing and developing a growing preschool ministry. For both Kent and Maria, the journey of leading and teaching preschoolers has just begun as they seek God's will in their lives and in their churches. Many other leaders and teachers around the world will join Kent and Maria in this journey. The work they do today will make a lasting impact on the church and the world well into the next century.

CHAPTER 2
Connecting with

"Where do I begin to learn about who preschoolers are, what they need, and how they learn?" asked Maria. "Just today, Adam, who is three, came to the door kicking and screaming. He finally made the transition from Dad's arms, and then he would not leave the arms of the teacher all morning. How can I meet his needs and teach him the Bible? How can I share the love of Jesus with him and his unsaved dad?"

Making the Connection

Think about the preschoolers in your class/department. How are they unique? In what ways are they alike?

Pray for each child and family in your class/department.

Understanding preschoolers is crucial to teaching them and meeting their needs. Preschoolers have many different backgrounds and situations, but they still have the same basic needs. These basic needs are love, trust, acceptance, independence, security, freedom, guidance, and a sense of accomplishment. While their environment has changed, the basic needs of preschoolers have not changed.

To a preschooler:

- **Love** is an action rather than an abstract feeling. A preschooler must feel loved to have his need for love met. A child expresses love as a result of how he has experienced love. When a teacher smiles, listens, hugs, or spends time with a child, she communicates love to the child.

- **Trust** is developed when needs are met regularly. Consistency is the key to successful trust-building. The trust that a child develops is the basis for faith and trust in Jesus when he is older. When a teacher feeds a baby or changes his diaper promptly, she communicates trust to the child.

- **Acceptance** grows from the unconditional love of parents and teachers. Because a child is made in God's image, she is worthy of acceptance and respect from the adults around her. When a teacher listens and gives a child undivided attention, he communicates his acceptance of the child.

Preschoolers

- **Independence** develops from being allowed to do things and make choices. A preschooler needs the opportunity to discover his unique gifts and abilities. When a teacher allows a child to complete a puzzle by himself, she fosters independence in the child.

- **Freedom** is learning to make appropriate choices. When parents and teachers guide a preschooler in making appropriate choices, they help the child develop independence or self-reliance. When a teacher provides several different learning centers/activities, she communicates freedom of choice to the preschooler.

- **Security** means providing a worry-free environment where the child knows he is welcome, safe, and free from harm. A preschooler feels secure when he sees the same teachers and children in the same room following a familiar routine. When a teacher is in the room to greet the child each Sunday, he helps a child feel secure.

- **Guidance** is direction given by a teacher to help the child make choices. A teacher guides through words, actions, and room arrangement. A teacher's responsibility is to guide the child to know how to care for himself, others, and property. Through positive guidance, teachers give a child the opportunity to learn right from wrong and make wise decisions on his own. The child begins to develop self-discipline through the teacher's guidance. When a teacher corrects a child's misbehavior by offering two positive options, she is redirecting the child and giving him an opportunity to make a wise choice.

- **A sense of accomplishment** results from having been given opportunities to succeed. As a child develops and learns new skills, she gains a sense of accomplishment through completing an activity. Teachers must provide activities that challenge yet do not frustrate a child. When a teacher provides both 7-piece and 12-piece puzzles in a class/department of three-year-olds, he provides an opportunity for each child to succeed at his own level.

Match each need with a statement.

___ Trust   A. You help me know the difference between what is right and wrong so that I can make good choices later.

___ Love   B. You let me make choices.

___ Acceptance   C. You provide activities that I can complete and that also challenge me.

___ Independence   D. You are kind and care about me.

___ Security   E. You let me do things by myself.

___ Freedom   F. I can depend on you to care for me.

___ Guidance   G. You respect me for who I am.

___ Sense of Accomplishment   H. You provide a safe place for me to play and are always here for me.

Checklist of ways a teacher can meet the needs of preschoolers:

- Pray daily for each child.
- Love all the preschoolers equally in a sincere, unconditional way.
- Provide an environment that is safe and secure.
- Give each child an opportunity to do all he can do for himself.
- Remind each child that he is special to you and to God.
- Always keep your promises and commitments.
- Treat each child with respect.
- Accept each child's abilities and special needs.
- Communicate to all parents the importance of understanding and meeting the needs of their preschoolers.
- Provide a routine schedule for consistency.
- Get to know each child's parents and their family needs.
- Accept cultural and economic differences.

"I have been observing the teachers in the baby department. Do you think they know how much babies can learn?" asked Kent.

"What do you mean?" said Rose.

"Last week, three-month-old Sarah came to church. Her Sunday School teacher said Sarah cries often and that she does not seem to be contented or satisfied. Sarah seems fearful when her diaper is changed and will not take her bottle without crying. The teacher also said that she only had time to meet physical needs, and she was not sure she could teach anything to a baby anyway. How can I help her know that babies can learn?"

Preschool leaders/teachers have known for a long time that holding, rocking, smiling, singing, cooing, and talking to a baby help the baby feel loved. Brain research has confirmed that when a baby is held, loved, and nurtured, the brain releases an important hormone necessary for growth. In her article "Fertile Minds" (*Time* magazine, February 3, 1997), Madeline Nash explains that babies are born with one hundred billion neurons. By the time the child is three, the brain has formed one thousand trillion connections, about twice as many neurons as adults have. Around age 10, the child's brain begins to get rid of the extra "connections" that are not used or stimulated. Nash writes: "Deprived of a stimulating environment, a child's brain suffers. Researchers at Baylor College of Medicine, for example, have found that children who don't play much or are rarely touched develop brains 20 to 30 percent smaller than normal for their age." Frank Newman, President of the Education Commission of the States, also notes, "There is a time scale to brain development, and the most important year is the first." Adults impact the learning of babies from the very beginning of life.

Making the Connection

What can you do to provide a stimulating environment for young preschoolers?

- Use Bible phrases as you meet the child's physical needs.
- Provide opportunities for the child to see, smell, taste, touch, and hear.
-
-
-

Maria sighed. "I just don't understand Tommy. He is at church every Sunday morning and every Wednesday night because his parents are involved in many ministries of the church. He's very active and is always getting into everything in the room. Why does he act this way?"

Each child is a unique creation of God, created with a sense of awe and wonder about the world around him. Though each child is unique, he exhibits some characteristics common to all preschoolers.

A preschooler is curious. She learns by using all her senses to

explore the world around her. She wonders how the world works and what objects do. She investigates the things that interest her. A four-year-old is constantly asking "Why?" in order to understand her world.

A preschooler is active. Physical activity is part of the natural growth of a child. Provide a teaching environment that allows preschoolers to move around the room. If a teacher asks a preschooler to sit still too long, learning may stop because all of the child's energy is focused on not moving.

A preschooler is creative. A child's imagination is enhanced when teachers provide an environment conducive to free expression. Giving a child a box of art supplies and blank paper rather than a coloring sheet allows the child to express her own ideas and feelings.

A preschooler is self-centered. He can think about the world only from his own point of view. He is not necessarily selfish but relates to everything from his own personal experience. A two-year-old may have difficulty sharing the puzzles in the room.

A preschooler is sensitive. Though she cannot verbalize her feelings, a preschooler can read the emotions and feelings around her. She needs a consistent, positive environment to help her grow. Without this type of environment, she may feel insecure and uncertain.

A preschooler has a limited attention span. His attention span is approximately one minute for each year of life. A child can only remain involved in an activity as long as his attention allows. A teacher encourages a child to work at his own pace by providing a variety of activities. The teacher allows the child to choose and move among those activities.

A preschooler is literal-minded. She thinks in terms of what she has seen and experienced. She understands words only in their concrete meanings. The use of symbolic language at home or church may confuse her. If a preschooler hears the phrase "You have grown another foot," she will look down to see where her new foot has grown.

A preschooler explores limits. A young child explores limits for two reasons. First, he wants greater independence. Second, he wants to be reassured that his environment is safe. As the child questions limits in his learning experiences, the teacher has opportunity to provide firm but loving guidance to ensure safety and a secure environment.

For age-specific characteristics, see pp. 19-21.

Spiritual Development

Spiritual growth in a preschooler is an increase in knowledge and understanding of God's love and care for her. From the first time a child comes to church, preschool leaders/teachers build foundations for spiritual growth. As teachers meet the child's physical and emotional needs, they communicate God's love to the child. As a child begins to trust her teachers, the spiritual foundation is laid. This simple foundation of trust in her physical surroundings will be the basis for later trust in Christ. The child will begin to associate positive feelings toward God and Jesus as she hears their names in relation to positive experiences at church. As a baby she may not know who Jesus is, but she will know that He is someone very special from the feelings and attitudes of her teachers. When teachers say Bible verses and sing songs, the child begins to associate the Bible with her world. The child begins to sense that the Bible is an important book for her. Adults must not miss opportunities to build on the spiritual foundations in the life of a child every time she comes to church. Quality baby-sitting may occur at every child-care facility in the city, but laying spiritual foundations in the life of a child sets the church apart from child care.

Making the Connection

How are you laying spiritual foundations in the lives of preschoolers?

What Bible phrases did you use in Sunday School this week?
1.
2.
3.

As preschoolers grow, teachers continue to build spiritual foundations. Preschoolers need to be taught Bible-based concepts about God and Jesus on their level of understanding. Activities should be child-oriented to engage the child in learning biblical truths. Each child needs to feel satisfaction from having participated in an activity with the teacher. The relationship built between teacher and child helps develop spiritual foundations. Teachers communicate the love of Jesus to the child by saying: "I am glad you came to church today. We have happy times as we learn about Jesus. Thank You, God, for my friend, Joey." A child who enjoys coming to church and learning in Sunday School will form positive attitudes toward church. He will see church as a place where people care about him and want to help him. These attitudes will carry over into adulthood, forming a foundation that will impact how the child views and understands the role of church in his life. Biblical and spiritual foundations last a lifetime. A Sunday School teacher is extremely important in shaping preschoolers' attitudes about spiritual matters.

The greatest influences in a preschooler's emotional, mental, social, and spiritual growth are his parents. Many parents take the task of raising their child seriously and are often overwhelmed. Although many of the parents do not see the need of being a part of church for themselves, they are looking for a place to take their children for moral and spiritual education. Preschool leaders and teachers must be willing to help educate parents about the spiritual development of their preschoolers and commit to partner with them in guiding the child to God.

Children with Special Needs

Kent greeted Jonathan and his parents as they walked into church. Jonathan is a three-year-old child with Down syndrome. Kent watched Jonathan and his parents walk down the hall. Kent wondered how his church could minister more effectively to Jonathan and his family.

Today, in almost every church, there are children with special needs. Some of those special needs result from an extremely short attention span, hyperactivity, Down syndrome, developmental delays, physical challenges, and sight and hearing impairments. Other special needs may arise for a child who is gifted. It is essential for preschool teachers to recognize and plan for the needs of all children. Trust should be built between parents and the preschool teachers so that the parents can have confidence that their child will be cared for appropriately. All parents need assurance that the

BONUS IDEA: When choosing resources for preschoolers with special needs, ask yourself these questions: Will this item be safe to use? Will the child experience success using it? Many preschoolers with special needs will enjoy sensory experiences using sand, water, play dough, and music.

teacher loves their children and is willing to seek information and advice from them in order to meet the needs of their children.

A teacher can take steps toward creating a successful, nurturing, teaching environment for a child with special needs:
- Meet with a child's parents to identify the child's abilities.
- Plan to meet with the child's parents when the child is not present.
- Arrange a convenient time to meet the parents away from the church.
- Enlist another teacher if necessary to help meet the needs of the class/department.
- Communicate regularly with the parents on progress, difficulties, or frustrations. Parents need to hear positive remarks regarding their children.
- Help parents locate a support group.
- Develop a child information sheet for teachers.
- Talk with other teachers that the child has or visit the school he attends.
- Find ways to adapt activities for the child with special needs.

Parents and teachers are a team and must work together for the best interest of the preschooler.

What are some special needs of the children in your department?

How are you meeting those needs?

Families of Other Cultures

Pastor Mike introduced Meiko and her parents to Maria. "Meiko's parents are students at the college here. Meiko speaks very little English."

As Maria guided Meiko into the room, she thought to herself, "Where do I begin to minister to this family?"

Preschool leaders/teachers have a biblical mandate in the Great Commission to reach the whole world. In many instances, "the world" has moved into neighborhoods near the church. Preschool leaders must be trained and encouraged to accept the similarities and differences of other cultures. Leaders and teachers may have the opportunity to impact the family and even the extended family far away.

Remember that children of a different cultural background have the same basic needs as all preschoolers. But they also have distinct needs that must be met. Consider these ideas for teaching preschoolers of various cultures.
- Visit in the child's home.
- Learn as much as possible about various cultures and customs.
- Give parents a list of common words that are used in the Sunday School.
- Learn a few key phrases in the child's language.
- Prepare activities based upon the child's interests, family, and culture.
- Use verbal and nonverbal cues for communicating.
- Use pictures to ask questions.
- Maintain eye contact when talking to the child.
- Avoid stereotypes.

Understanding the characteristics and needs of preschoolers will enable leaders and teachers to make a difference in the lives of preschoolers today and into the 21st Century.

Babies

Spiritual
- develop a sense of trust as needs are met consistently
- sense attitudes and expressions of love
- learn to associate God's name with love and trust
- sense importance associated with Jesus and the Bible
- may point to the Bible and pictures of Jesus

Social/Emotional
- show alertness when talked to
- smile broadly at others
- begin to initiate social interchange
- become quiet in unfamiliar settings
- make eye contact
- are interested in other children

Mental
- use senses to learn
- cry to signal pain or distress
- recognize principle caregivers
- use vocal and nonvocal communication
- react differently to familiar and unfamiliar
- know and respond to name

Physical
- use many complex reflexes
- begin to reach toward objects
- hold up their heads
- sit without support
- roll over, crawl
- look for dropped toys

Ones

Spiritual
- begin to make simple choices
- continue to grow in trust of adults
- begin to distinguish between acceptable and unacceptable behavior
- begin to recognize simple pictures of Jesus

Social/Emotional
- experience stranger anxiety
- play simple games
- can practice "taking turns"
- like to exert control
- recognize others' emotions
- imitate household actions

Mental
- remember simple events
- begin to group familiar objects
- use trial and error in learning
- can label body parts
- understand and use words for items
- try to make self understood

Physical
- sit well in chairs
- climb
- love to explore
- use markers on paper
- carry objects from place to place
- move constantly

Twos

Spiritual
- can sing simple songs about God and Jesus
- can say thank you to God
- can listen to Bible stories

Social/Emotional
- take interest in family
- try to help
- initiate play with peers
- can be loving and affectionate
- are responsive to others' moods
- use imagination
- strongly assert independence

Mental
- use 5-300 words
- begin using sentences
- identify self by gender
- follow simple directions in order
- match, compare, group, sort items
- enjoy repetition
- begin using numbers
- repeat songs
- know colors

Physical
- develop preference for right or left hand
- stand on one foot and balance
- jump on tiptoes
- walk between parallel lines
- have better gross-motor coordination
- have difficulty relaxing
- help undress self

Threes

Spiritual
- can identify some Bible characters and stories
- recognize the Bible as a special book; enjoy handling and using the Bible
- enjoy singing songs about Bible friends, family, nature, friends at church
- understand that God, Jesus, and church are special
- try to please adults
- begin to develop a conscience and are sensitive to feelings of shame and guilt

Social/Emotional
- try to please adults; conform more often
- begin to show some self-control, but resort to temper tantrums when extremely angry
- take turns more readily
- like to hear self talk
- respond to verbal guidance and enjoy encouragement
- play cooperatively with others
- have imaginary companions

Mental
- use 300-1000 words
- learn short songs
- display creativity and imagination
- experience fears and bad dreams
- begin speaking in complete sentences
- can only do one thing at a time
- want to know what things are and how they work

Physical
- use large muscles
- dress self fairly easily
- display some fine motor skills
- notice the differences in boys and girls
- dislike nap time and cannot sleep during this time

Fours

Spiritual
- like to retell Bible stories
- enjoy Bible-verse games
- recognize that God and Jesus love people and help people in special ways
- accept responsibility for helping people
- exhibit a conscience

Social/Emotional
- have total confidence in own abilities
- are bossy; show great independence
- tattle frequently
- focus on cooperative play and take turns
- like to be helpers if they initiate the idea
- respond to reason, humor, and firmness

Mental
- can remember name and address
- have increased attention span
- can do two things at once
- are highly imaginative; cannot separate fact and fantasy
- show a curiosity about life cycle
- understand time concepts better
- use 500-2000 words
- enjoy being silly

Physical
- show good large muscle coordination
- develop a longer, leaner body
- develop fine motor control for cutting with scissors, painting, and drawing
- walk backwards
- need a high level of physical activity

Pre-Ks

Spiritual
- begin to ask questions about God
- express love for God and Jesus
- can recall simple Bible stories
- can make life application of Bible verses
- may show concern for others
- can sing songs about Jesus
- continue to develop a conscience

Social/Emotional
- play cooperatively with other children
- enjoy imitating adults
- begin to distinguish truth from lies
- enjoy competition
- are learning to share and take turns
- can accept responsibility

Mental
- are challenged by new tasks
- seek explanations concerning why and how
- begin to recognize basic reading words
- enjoy classification, sequencing, and sorting
- use many words without knowing their meanings
- use a vocabulary of 2000 plus words

Physical
- have good eye-hand coordination
- dress self
- exhibit right and left handedness
- can control their large muscles
- enjoy building materials with parts to assemble
- develop appetites for favorite foods
- are learning to print and copy words

Kindergartners

Spiritual
- remember and like to tell Bible stories
- use the Bible and like to find Bible phrases/verses
- like to know they are doing what the Bible says
- sing songs about God and Jesus
- try to help and love other people
- like to take care of God's world
- continue developing a conscience
- express guilt for misbehavior

Social/Emotional
- get along well in small groups
- comfort friends who are upset
- have best friends, but change friends often
- like to please adults
- may be prone to self-criticism and guilt
- enjoy group play
- play easy games with a friend, following rules
- may continue to express fears

Mental
- can print name, but not too clearly
- know colors and shapes
- can name most uppercase letters
- can read a few words
- utilize a 2000-word vocabulary
- say numbers 1 to 20
- know morning from afternoon
- hear the beginning sounds of words

Physical
- skip well; hop in a straight line
- display good eye-hand coordination
- cut well with scissors
- exhibit well-established right or left handedness
- begin cutting permanent teeth
- dress and undress well alone
- girls may display more maturity than boys

CHAPTER 3
Connecting Through

Best practices are recommendations that will enable leaders and teachers to build a strong Sunday School.

A million thoughts were running through Kent's head. "Wow! There is a whole lot more to teaching Sunday School than just the Sunday morning experience." Kent began to make a list of the things that needed to be considered in providing quality learning experiences for preschoolers. His list included organizing and grouping of preschoolers, record keeping, Extended Teaching Care, room arrangements, utilization and sharing of space, policies and procedures, equipment, and leadership meetings.

"Where do I begin?" he thought. "What is the greatest need of my Preschool Division?" Deciding how to group and organize the preschool area seemed to be the best place to start.

Organization is the key to an effective preschool ministry, whether the church is small, medium, or large. An effective preschool class, department, or division is organized with consideration of what is best practice for preschoolers. Preschoolers should be grouped according to age and developmental stage. In grouping preschoolers, several factors need to be considered. They are:

- number of preschoolers enrolled and number of prospects;
- number of teachers—for safety reasons, there should be a minimum of two adults in a room;
- space available for preschool classrooms; and
- additional teacher for each child who has special needs.

Planning

The following models offer best practices for organizing preschool Sunday School. Choose the model that best fits your church.

Model One	Model Two	Model Three	Model Four
All preschoolers in one class (no more than 12 including teachers)	Birth—Twos Threes—Kindergarten	Babies Ones—Twos Threes—Pre-K Kindergarten	Babies Ones Twos Threes Fours—Pre-K Kindergarten

Each model offers strengths. **Multi-age classes** create a family-like atmosphere. Younger children can learn from observing older preschoolers. Older preschoolers have opportunities to help younger preschoolers and the teacher.

Narrower age span classes are designed so that activities meet the unique needs and abilities of the age group. In any preschool class/department, teachers can provide fun activities that engage preschoolers in learning Bible truths.

As you consider your class/department needs, it is important to keep proper teacher/child ratios. Proper ratios in each class/department allow the teachers time to

meet needs and develop relationships with each preschooler in their care. The number of preschoolers in a department and the ratio of teachers to preschoolers are determined by the age of the preschoolers. Use the following chart to help determine the number of departments you need to keep the proper teacher/child ratio.

Age	Recommended Enrollment*	Teachers	Maximum Enrollment
Babies—Kindergarten	9	3	12
Babies—Twos	9	3	12
Threes—Kindergarten	12	3	15
Babies	8	4	12
Ones—Twos	9	3	12
Threes—Pre-K	16	4	20
Kindergarten	20	4	24

*Includes prospects

Draw a chart of what your preschool organization should look like.

Another way of determining your organizational needs is to use the following chart. Locate the year and month in which a child is born to determine the class/department for the child. The chart will vary according to the kindergarten requirement for your community.

Age Group Chart
2000 - 2001

	JAN	FEB	MAR	APR	MAY	JUNE	JULY	AUG.	SEPT	OCT	NOV	DEC
2000												
1999						BABIES- Room 121						
1998				ONES - Room 122								
1997				TWOS - Room 123								
1996				THREES- Room 124								
1995				FOURS/PRE-K - Room 125								
1994				KINDERGARTEN - Room 126								
1993												

(A reproducible blank chart can be found on p. 33.)

Children remain in the same class/department for the entire church year. Babies and ones are usally the exceptions and are promoted according to development rather than age. **Avoid moving a child more than once during a church year.**

Consider a new best practice: At the beginning of the church year, if space allows, establish classes/departments with full enrollment. Leave vacant rooms for new classes/departments to be created as babies are born or prospects come. As babies develop, recreate the room to meet their needs such as removing rocking chairs and cribs. This will encourage trust for both parents and children and allow leaders to develop relationships for a full year.

Keeping and maintaining good records of members and prospects will help preschool leaders minister more effectively to preschoolers and their families. Effective records can help alert leaders to the need to expand their preschool classes, departments, or division.

Guidelines for starting a new preschool class or department are:
- babies through kindergartners are in one class and more than 12 are enrolled in the class;
- babies are in the same department as older preschoolers;
- kindergartners are in the same class with younger preschoolers;
- class or department exceeds the recommended teacher/child ratios;
- class or department provides only baby-sitting; or
- prospects outnumber preschoolers enrolled.

When do you make the decision to move to multiple Sunday Schools? A church may need multiple Sunday Schools when its buildings no longer accommodate the number of people participating in Sunday School. Multiple Sunday Schools provide an opportunity to reach more preschoolers and their families by creating new classes/departments.

When planning for multiple Sunday School preschool leaders, Sunday School teachers, and ETC teachers need to make the following decisions:
- Decide on use of space, equipment, and supplies
- Agree on room arrangement, supplies, equipment, and storage
- Develop procedures for receiving and dismissing preschoolers
- Develop a plan for coordinating the arrangement and the use of rooms.
- Budget for additional curriculum, resources, supplies, and equipment.
- Enlist leaders for the additional hour of Sunday School.
- Provide time for leadership meetings for both Sunday School ministries.
- Plan for increased traffic in preschool areas.
- Determine how attendance will be counted.
- Plan how transitions between sessions can be smooth and comfortable for preschoolers, parents, and teachers.

Need help with age group and grading? Check out the Preschool Curriculator on our Web site at www.lifeway.com/presource.

Maria noticed that the session after Sunday School seemed very disorganized.

"Preschoolers are always learning at church," she thought. "They need to be involved in quality learning experiences each time they are here. What can we do to help the teaching session during worship service?"

See *ETC: A Lasting Impression (A Handbook for Coordinating Extended Teaching Care)* for more information on organizing and coordinating ETC.

Why use carpet? It's warmer, quieter, and more comfortable.

Why use tile? It's better for messy activities and easier to keep clean.

SOME OPTIONS
Babies Through Twos
- Tile with solid vinyl mats
- Fire retardant carpet with solid vinyl mats

Threes Through Kindergartners
- Combination of tile and fire retardant carpet

Extended Teaching Care (ETC)

ETC (Extended Teaching Care) involves caring and teaching for preschoolers during the worship service. ETC is often a visiting family's first and last impression of the preschool ministries of a church. ETC can be provided for all preschoolers (birth—kindergartners) or for selected ages of preschoolers (birth—threes) to encourage older preschoolers (fours and older) to attend worship service with their families. A well-planned and implemented ETC ministry is crucial.

Who is responsible for ETC? The entire church has a responsibility for the ETC ministry. Someone must coordinate the ETC ministry. ETC may be coordinated by an enlisted ETC coordinator, the Preschool Division director, the preschool minister or minister of education, the preschool committee members, the preschool Sunday School department directors, or the Sunday School Council or Sunday School Leadership Team.

What does a coordinator do? The coordinator enlists, schedules, and trains teachers. She sends reminders or calls ETC teachers early each week, assists in locating teaching materials, provides snacks, assists with schedule changes, refers teachers to substitutes, and is available during ETC to assist as needed. She determines a rotation plan that serves the church, and she distributes a roster of teachers' names, telephone numbers, and assigned dates.

How often do teachers serve? Teachers may volunteer one Sunday a month, one Sunday a quarter, consecutive Sundays in a month, or at other intervals. The more consistent and simple the plan, the easier it is for teachers to remember and for them to meet the needs of the preschoolers.

Where do I find teachers? A minimum of two teachers is needed in each room. Use the recommended Sunday School ratios (see p. 24). Schedule a few extra teachers each Sunday to fill gaps. Potential volunteers include parents of children in ETC, preschool Sunday School teachers, grandparents, senior adults, median adults, newlyweds, single adults, college students, preschool committee members, and deacons. Use a church survey, the church directory, Vacation Bible School faculty list, and church membership roll to find teachers.

Guidelines for Preschool Space

As Kent and Rose walked through the preschool area, Kent commented, "We need a few new classrooms."

"What are some things we need to think about as we look for new space?" Rose asked.

Another important factor in preschool organization is the space available for preschoolers. The best preschool teaching takes place in an area where the developmental characteristics and needs of the age group are given consideration.

Some guidelines are:

Size of Room
35 square feet per child

Doors
- Solid with small rectangular window for safety and security (Half doors are not recommended; they invite teachers to visit with others in the hallway, and children are distracted by movement and noise outside the open half door.)
- Open to the outside of the room
- 36 inches wide (A crib could pass through in the event of an emergency.)

Floors —Whatever choice is made, cleanliness is important.
- Allow preschoolers the freedom to participate in a variety of activities
- Comfortable
- Clean
- Safe

Electrical Outlets—NOTE: In rooms for babies through twos, outlets should be 4½ feet from the floor.
- Two per wall
- Safety outlets or safety covers

Sink and Cabinet
- Babies through twos rooms—adult height (36 inches)
- Threes through kindergarten rooms—adult height (36 inches); child-height sink (27 inches)

Walls
- Color
  - Neutral colors or soft pastels are best.
  - For rooms which receive much natural light, soft blues and other "cool" colors work well.
  - For rooms which receive little or no natural light, a "warm" color such as soft yellow is a good choice.

NOTE: Bold colors, patterns, chair rails, borders, and murals may distract from learning, make rooms look cluttered, or encourage over active behavior. A good compromise is adding a soft color accent wall to the room.
- Type of covering
  - Washable, nontoxic paint
  - Vinyl wallpaper with no pattern

Ceilings
Acoustical ceilings (These ceilings work to keep down the noise level.)

Windows
- 18 inches from the floor to provide preschoolers a better view of God's world
- Window ledges flush with the wall
- Miniblinds, when necessary, to eliminate glare or to close out distractions
- Shatterproof glass

Lighting
Fluorescent lighting
  - Brighter
  - Less expensive

TOY TIP: Avoid using dolls with rooted hair. A plastic doll with molded hair is washable and more functional for preschoolers.

NOTE: In rooms designed for babies, lights should be on a dimmer switch or designed so that the lights on one side of the room can be turned on while leaving the lights off on the other side of the room.

Rest Rooms
- Connected to the department
- Child-sized toilets
- Sinks with paper towels and soap dispenser on the level of preschoolers inside the department room
- Tile floors
- Doors without locks

Choosing the Right Crib
Hospital cribs are recommended but expensive. Commercial portable cribs are an acceptable substitute. When purchasing or using donated cribs, consider the following guidelines:
- Slats should be no more than 2⅜ inches apart.
- Distance from the top of the mattress to the top of the rail should be at least 36 inches.
- Mattress should fit snugly in the crib.
- Corner posts should be no more than 1/16 inch.
- Any cutouts in headboard or footboard should be too small to allow head entrapment.
- Drop-side latches should be secure.
- Crib can fit through the door (for emergency evacuation).

Avoid stackable cribs. The closeness of several babies contributes to the spread of disease. Also, stackable cribs encourage too many babies in a small space.

Criteria for Selecting Toys for Preschool Rooms
- No sharp edges or points
- Suitable for age and development of child
- No small objects that can be removed and swallowed
- No mechanisms that can pinch or trap a child's fingers
- Washable
- Made of nonflammable materials
- Challenging, but not frustrating for children

Selecting Equipment for Preschool Rooms
A preschool room should contain equipment and furniture that will enhance the Bible teaching environment. The equipment and furniture selected will be used by all areas of preschool ministry and must meet the needs of the preschoolers who use the room. Each age group requires different types of equipment for appropriate teaching.

Good preschool teaching can occur with limited supplies and equipment. When space or budget are limited, teachers can choose the equipment or furniture that is most needed. Other items can be added when space or funds are available.

A recommended equipment chart is located on pp. 34-35.

Room Arrangement
The placement of equipment, furniture, and resources is important to creating a positive learning environment. A good arrangement helps ensure the best use of the room and enhances learning. Consider these guidelines:
- Place the homeliving/dramatic play across the room from the door.

> To encourage teachers to give their full attention to teaching Bible truths, provide audio cassettes of worship services rather than expensive speakers in preschool rooms.

- Group quiet activities together.
- Arrange more active, noisy activities near each other.
- Locate "messy" activities near a water source or rest room.
- Place nature materials near a window.
- To create space in a room, use the floor for some activities.

See the appendix for sample room arrangements for each age grouping.

Developing Preschool Policies and Procedures

Pastor Mike saw Maria walking quickly down the hall. "What's wrong, Maria?" he asked.

"I'm looking for Keisha's mother," Maria said. "Keisha has a fever. She was sick all week, but her mother really wanted her to come to church today. I wish we had a way to help parents know when their children may need to stay home."

Kent overheard teachers talking in a ones department.

"I don't know why we should have to wear gloves," one said. "They never wear gloves in that other department. I think our department director is just trying to make our job more difficult."

Developing preschool policies can be very helpful to a preschool ministry. Any preschool class, department, or division can implement procedures for consistent care. Whether large or small, a church should have basic written policies to guide the preschool ministry. Policies can be developed by a preschool committee or a group of teachers, parents, and church leaders. Each church's policies will reflect the individual needs and ministry of the church. Policies:
- help communicate to everyone basic policy procedures;
- give direction to help teachers respond consistently to situations; and
- explain hygiene and cleanliness, illness, use of preschool rooms, safety and security, reporting abuse, and emergency procedures.

Sample Policies and Procedures

Hygiene Policies
1. Infants will be diapered in their cribs. Older babies and ones will be changed on a nonporous surface. This surface will be sanitized after each use. Waxed paper will be used underneath soiled diapers.
2. Teachers will wear disposable gloves when changing a diaper or assisting a child with toileting needs. A new set of gloves is required for each diaper.
3. Disposable gloves will be worn when performing any first-aid procedures.
4. Handwashing prevents the spread of infection. Children should wash their hands after they use the toilet, wipe eyes or nose, and before eating or serving snacks. Teachers, also, will wash their hands often.
5. A disinfecting solution made of ¼ cup household bleach to 1 gallon of water will be used for wiping up all spills, cleaning diaper-changing areas, washing hands, and cleaning all toys and equipment. Disinfecting solution should be made for each session to ensure effectiveness. After a session, discard the solution.

BONUS IDEA:
Plan an annual "Meet Your Roommate" fellowship for all organizations who use preschool rooms. Teachers can discuss and decide how space and resources will be shared.

General Policies
1. The preschool facilities are available only when supervised by authorized personnel.
2. Children may be left in a preschool room only when a parent or another responsible adult is participating in church services or church-sponsored activities.
3. All personal items (such as bottles, diaper bags, extra clothing, etc.) should be labeled with the child's first and last name.
4. Bottles will be warmed slowly and in a manner that ensures they are safe for children to drink (such as in a slow cooker with water). No bottles will be warmed with a microwave oven.
5. Personal toys and games should be left at home. Security items are acceptable.
6. Parents of preschoolers will be asked to teach in ETC (Extended Teaching Care). Assignments are made on a rotating basis.

Security
1. Preschoolers are registered at the door using the sign-in sheet. Parents are to indicate where they can be located in case of an emergency.
2. Parents are given permanent identification cards which must be presented when they pick up their children.

Suggestions to Parents
To make your child's experiences at church happy and meaningful, you can:
1. Bring your child to church regularly. Talk about church and the happy experiences you have there.
2. Dress your child comfortably.
3. Allow adequate time for dressing and feeding your child before coming to church.
4. Encourage your child to walk with you to the room. This provides a sense of independence.
5. Always say good-bye to your child before you leave. Assure your child that you will return later.
6. Leave promptly, even if your child seems fretful. If your child remains unhappy for an extended time, the teacher will come and get you.

Reception and Dismissal
1. Preschoolers are received 15 minutes before each session and should be picked up immediately following each church activity.
2. To ensure safety, only preschoolers and teachers should be inside the classroom. Knock at the door and wait for a teacher to receive or dismiss the child.
3. A child should not be left in a preschool room unless a teacher is present.
4. Preschoolers are brought to their classes by and released to a parent or adult guardian who presents the permanent security card.

Illness Policy
1. Parents are asked not to bring their child to a church program or function if any of the following conditions exist:
   - temperature of 100 degrees in the last 24 hours
   - vomiting
   - diarrhea
   - severe coughing
   - pink eye
   - head lice
   - undiagnosed rash
   - open skin lesions
   - any symptoms of infectious childhood disease

2. Children who appear ill during a church session will be isolated with supervision, and the parents will be expected to come for the child.
3. If a child contracts a childhood disease following a session in a preschool department, the church should be notified.

Guidelines for Reporting Suspected Child Abuse
1. Document all efforts at handling the incident.
2. Report the incident immediately to the church's insurance company, attorney, and appropriate church staff.
3. Contact the appropriate civil authorities.
4. Notify the parents.
5. Do not confront the accused until the safety of the child is secured.

Planning for Ministry

The best learning experiences for preschoolers occur when the leadership has been involved in planning and preparation. Leadership planning helps ensure that:

- learning centers are prepared and the room is set up before the session begins;
- Bible truths are taught through the use of Bible-learning centers/activities, Bible phrases and verses, and Bible stories;
- preschoolers have choices because more than one activity has been planned;
- ministry, outreach, and evangelism are given priority;
- training opportunities are planned and encouraged for all leaders; and
- preschool leaders feel they have contributed to the total work of preschool Sunday School and to the work of the church.

Leadership Planning Meetings
The leadership planning meeting helps all Sunday School teachers be more effective in all aspects of Sunday School ministry. The meeting provides a regular time for Sunday School leaders to focus on the mission of the church and how Sunday School in general, and their classes/departments in particular, are working to fulfill that mission. In a leadership meeting, leaders can evaluate their relationships with people, both members and prospects, and evaluate the Bible teaching and learning that are taking place. Weekly leadership meetings are recommended, but some churches may find that monthly meetings are more suitable.

What happens in a leadership meeting?
General Period—*(15 minutes)* During this period, all Sunday School leaders gather to discuss the Sunday School ministry. The Sunday School director, pastor, or minister of education motivate and inform leaders about concerns related to the Sunday School ministry.
Class/Department Leadership Meeting—Leaders of each class or department discuss specific concerns of their class/department. The meeting is divided into three areas:
Focus on the Mission (10 minutes)—Leaders relate the work of the class/department to the mission and ministry of the church and the Sunday School ministry. Leaders are made aware of churchwide emphases, needs, and concerns and how the Sunday School can support or address them.
Focus on Relationships (25 minutes)—Leaders focus on relationships with members and prospects. Individual needs are assessed and plans are made to respond to them. Specific plans are made for following up on ministry needs. Plans are made for fellowship activities involving preschoolers and their families. Visitation assignments and reports can be shared. Other outreach activities can also be planned or reported.

Focus on Bible Study (25 minutes)—Leaders discuss how to teach Bible truths to preschoolers effectively. Leaders can evaluate past teaching sessions and discuss changes that need to be made. They can discuss the learning needs of children and determine how to meet those needs. Leaders plan Bible-teaching activities and make assignments for upcoming sessions.

Division Planning

When a church has several preschool classes/departments, planning together as a division can be helpful. Division planning may include:
- establishing goals for preschool Sunday School;
- determining how the Preschool Division supports the total church ministry;
- planning Vacation Bible School, fellowships, training events, and other church events; and/or
- working though issues such as sharing space or preschool policies.

Annual Planning

Annual planning helps develop the overall Sunday School ministry and gives direction to each class/department. During annual planning, leaders can evaluate what is happening in Sunday School, identify priorities for the coming year, set goals, and plan actions toward meeting goals. Annual planning can be an effective tool to create teamwork among Sunday School classes/departments of all ages. (For more information on annual planning, see *Sunday School for a New Century*.)

> **ROOM TIP:** Younger preschoolers need a teacher's full attention. Avoid placing speakers in preschool rooms.

> **Preschool Committee**
>
> Kent and Maria met at a state training conference. As they talked together, they recognized that, though their churches were very different, they shared some common needs and concerns.
>
> "I wish we had someone to help us with all those details about preschool Sunday School," Maria said.
>
> "I know," said Kent. "I could use some help in our preschool ministry, too."

A preschool committee can help make decisions for implementing a quality preschool ministry. Parents, teachers, and other interested adults can be enlisted to serve on the committee. In addition to making the decisions, the preschool committee gives support to the preschool ministry among the church congregation. The committee may have as few as 3 members or as many as 10 members. All committee members must be dedicated to sound preschool Bible teaching. A preschool committee can:
- help develop and implement policies;
- recommend the purchase of equipment, furniture, and supplies;
- coordinate space usage;
- develop organization of the preschool ministry; and
- oversee the administration of preschool Sunday School.

Planning and organizing a preschool Sunday School ministry can be challenging. Organization is necessary, whether the preschool ministry is one department or several age-group divisions. Organization impacts teaching, and effective planning makes Bible teaching more effective.

Age Group Chart

	Jan.	Feb.	Mar.	Apr.	May	June	July	Aug.	Sept.	Oct.	Nov.	Dec.

Recommended Preschool

Symbols:
x recommended
o optional

The all column is specialized equipment that a church may want to purchased in limited quantity (1 or 2 per church) for use by all ages.

Equipment	B	1	2	3	4	K	All	B-2	3-K	B-K
General										
Rest mats or towels		x	o					x		o
Cribs (hospital 27"x42")	x	o						x		x
Adult rocking chair (2)	x							x		x
Solid surface floor mat (42" x 42")	x									
Wall cabinet (50" above floor)	x	x	x	x	x	x		x	x	x
Trash receptacles with lid	x	x	x	x	x	x		x	x	x
Diaper bag cubbies or hooks	x	x	x							
Vinyl changing pad		x	x							
Open shelf/closed back for toys (26"x36"x12")		o						o		o
Child safety gate										o
Water source for disinfecting	x	x	x					x		x
Slow cookers	x							x		x
Folding screen for nursing area	x							x		x
Rocking boat with enclosed steps		o								
Small counter top refrigerator	o									
Homeliving/Dramatic Play										
Horizontal unbreakable mirror 24" x 48" attached to wall	x							o		
Vertical unbreakable mirror 24" x 48" attached to wall		x	x	x	x				o	o
Wooden doll bed (16" x 28" x 8")		o	x	x	x			x	x	x
Child size rocker		o	x	x	x				x	x
Table (24"x36"x22")		x	x							
Table (24"x36"x24")				x	x				x	x
2-4 chairs (10")		x	x							
2-4 chairs (12"-14")				x	x				x	x
Wooden sink		x	x	x	x				x	x
Wooden stove		x	x	x	x				x	x
Chest of drawers							o			
Child size ironing board and iron							o			
Music										
Cassette tape/CD player	x	x	x	x	x	x		o	o	o
Autoharp							x			
Rhythm instruments							x			

Equipment

Equipment	B	1	2	3	4	K	All	B-2	3-K	B-K
Blocks										
Cardboard or vinyl blocks		X	X					X		
Wooden unit blocks (various shapes and sizes)										
1. 29-70 pieces				X					X	X
2. 100-150 pieces					X	X				
Open shelf/closed back (26"x36"x12")			O	X	X	X			X	X
Art										
Table (30"x48"x22")		X	X						X	X
Table (30"x48"x24")				X	X					
2-4 chairs (10")		X	X							
2-4 chairs (12"-14")				X	X				O	O
Art Easel/ adjustable legs *				X	X	X	X		O	O
Drying rack				X	X	X	X			
Water source at child's height for clean up				X	X	X	X		X	X
Art shelf (36"x46"x16")						X				
Nature/Science										
Open shelf with closed back (26"x30"x12")				X	X	X			O	O
Water table (1 per church)							O			
Table (24"x36"x24")							O			
2-4 chairs (12"-14")							O			
Manipulatives/Puzzles										
Puzzle rack				O	O	O			O	O
Table (24"x36"x24")							O			
2-4 chairs (12"-14")							O			

Maximum number of 2 tables per room in 2-4 year old rooms.
*One option for art easels would be to have 1 easel per every three rooms.

CHAPTER 4
Connecting with

Kent picked up the phone as it rang for a third time. "Hello?"

"Hi, Kent," a pleasant voice said. "This is Dennis. I'm chairperson of the nominating committee. Did you get the list I sent you?"

"Yes," Kent replied. "I see a few openings for preschool leaders."

Dennis chuckled. "Do you know any friends who owe you a favor?"

"Maybe I could twist a few arms," Kent laughed. "But seriously, teaching preschoolers is important. Just the other day, Deborah told me what happened in her department. Marianna and her family visited our church. Marianna pointed to a picture of Jesus and asked, 'Who is that man?' Deborah told me she later thanked God for letting her introduce Marianna to Jesus. We need to find more teachers excited about introducing preschoolers to Jesus. Where are we going to find teachers like that?"

Dennis said, "Let's begin to pray together now that God will help us find the leaders He has prepared."

All good preschool teachers are dedicated to teaching the children. They begin when the first child arrives, and they do not stop until the last child leaves. Just as preschoolers have certain basic characteristics, so do good preschool teachers.

A preschool teacher is:
- a growing Christian, committed to teaching Sunday School seven days a week. Teachers regularly study the Bible and live out its teachings in their lives.
- an active member of the church for more than six months. Teachers have a positive attitude about the church and are involved in and support the ministry of the church.
- called by God and dependent upon God and the Holy Spirit. Teachers feel that God has led them to make a difference in preschoolers' lives.
- ready to tell parents about Jesus. Teachers know how to lead people to Christ.
- committed to the purpose of Sunday School. Teachers understand the functions of the church and the role of Sunday School in fulfilling the Great Commission.

Leadership

- committed to planning and building biblical foundations in the lives of preschoolers. Teachers have regularly scheduled planning meetings.
- cooperative, dependable, and flexible. Teachers adapt as needed.
- willing to learn more about preschoolers and preschool ministry. Teachers participate regularly in training to prepare to be the best leaders they can be.
- comfortable with preschoolers and genuinely loves them. Teachers like being around preschoolers and are sensitive to the different needs of preschoolers.

Even though preschool teachers have the same basic characteristics, no two are exactly alike. A teacher's unique God-given spiritual gifts and talents allow her to be the individual God created her to be. "When Christians serve in their area of giftedness, they generally function less in their own strength and more in the power of the Holy Spirit. Thus, ordinary people can accomplish the 'extraordinary.'"[1] Extraordinary is just what preschool teachers are!

Describe your calling to teach preschoolers.

What experiences and talents do you bring to teaching preschoolers?

Enlisting preschool teachers is a continuous process. Church leaders always should be alert and sensitive to the Holy Spirit's direction for the preschool ministry team. Where can potential leaders and teachers be found?

- Adult Sunday School rolls
- Church directory and church membership roll
- Vacation Bible School faculty list
- Potential leader training class
- Interest surveys
- Former teachers
- New member surveys (enlist a new member after six months)
- ETC (Extended Teaching Care) teachers

A teacher should be enlisted by the person to whom she will be directly responsible. When enlisting potential preschool teachers, consider the following steps:

1. Pray.
2. Make initial contact to set up a time to meet one-on-one.
3. During the visit, share qualifications and specific expectations (ministry description), curriculum, and age-group characteristics.
4. Explain screening procedures.
5. Answer any questions.
6. Pray together.
7. Set a time for follow-up.
8. Follow up on previous visit.
9. Accept the answer.[2]

A ministry description lists the responsibilities of each preschool leader. Leaders in the Preschool Division include a division director, a division outreach-evangelism director, a department director for each preschool class/department, and one or more teachers for each preschool class/department. Other leaders may be enlisted for the division or department as determined by the church.

Responsibilities of the Division Director

The division director is responsible to the Sunday School director for the total ministry of the Preschool Sunday School Division. The division director:

- meets regularly with the Sunday School Council.
- coordinates work of the Preschool Division and develops the organization.
- discovers, enlists, and trains new preschool leaders and teachers.
  - evaluates, encourages, affirms, and directs preschool leaders and teachers.
    - meets regularly with leaders and teachers for planning and evaluation.

- oversees the coordination of FIRST CONTACT.
- evaluates the needs of the division and recommends actions related to space, budget, curriculum, supplies, and other resources.
- sets a positive example by living as an authentic witness of Christ and through full involvement in the ministry of the church.

Responsibilities of the Division Outreach-Evangelism Director

The division outreach-evangelism director works with the division director and the general outreach-evangelism director to lead the Preschool Division in outreach and evangelism. The division outreach-evangelism director:

- serves as a FAITH Group Leader or Team Leader (for churches using FAITH: Sunday School Evangelism Strategy).
- coordinates all evangelism and outreach activities and prospect-discovery efforts for the Preschool Division.
- assists in training preschool leaders and teachers in evangelism and outreach.
- promotes outreach and evangelism objectives with leaders and teachers.
- maintains active prospect records for the Preschool Division.
- greets visiting preschool families and assists in locating the appropriate preschool departments.
- coordinates FIRST CONTACT or works closely with the coordinator to make sure that families of infants are contacted regularly.
- sets a positive example by living as an authentic witness of Christ and through full involvement in the ministry of the church.

Responsibilities of the Department Director

A department director is responsible to the division director for the total ministry of a preschool class/department. A preschool department director:

- leads in planning and administering the total work of the class/department.
- meets regularly with teachers for prayer, planning, and making assignments related to evangelism and outreach, fellowship, ministry, and Bible teaching.
- greets preschoolers and families when they arrive.
- serves as lead teacher for the class/department, directing overall teaching learning experiences.
- leads group learning experiences (for children three years old and older
- maintains general records for the class/department. (Some classes/departments may choose to enlist a secretary to assist in record keeping and tasks. For a complete job description for department secretary, see *Sunday School for a New Century*.)
- evaluates the needs of the class/department and recommends actions related to space, budget, curriculum, supplies, and other resources.
- sets a positive example by living as an authentic witness of Christ and through full involvement in the ministry of the church.

Responsibilities of the Teacher

A teacher invests himself in building positive relationships with preschoolers and involves preschoolers in meaningful Bible-learning experiences. A preschool teacher:

- prepares and leads Bible-learning centers/activities for foundational Bible teaching.
- builds positive relationships with preschoolers and families.
- contacts members, prospects, and families regularly to meet needs.
- leads parents toward faith in Jesus Christ and guides them to serve Him through worship, evangelism, fellowship, discipleship, and ministry.
- sets a positive example by living as an authentic witness of Christ and through full involvement in the ministry of the church.

All Christians are called to minister. The word "minister" means servant. Christians are taught to serve God and minister to others.[3] Teaching preschoolers is a part of the ministering process. A teacher needs to have a good balance of reaching new preschoolers and their parents and of nurturing the preschoolers already involved. The relationship that a teacher has with the parents of preschoolers is one of great significance in meeting the needs of each child. Communication between parents and teachers is vital. Working together, parents and teachers can help the child become all God intends for him to be. A good relationship between parents and teachers enhances the ministry to families of preschoolers with special needs. A caring relationship can open many hearts and doors of opportunity.

Leadership conferences are provided each summer for all church leaders. Contact LifeWay Christian Resources or see LifeWay Online (www. lifeway.com) for a list of conferences and dates at each conference center.

Making the Connection

List leadership responsibilities you have in your class, department, or division.

"When I went to the associational leadership training conference," said Kent, "I heard about doing background checks on anyone who is in contact with preschoolers, children, or youth in churches."

"How do we get started?" asked Rose.

When teachers are enlisted, they should be asked to participate in the church's volunteer screening program. The screening of teachers has arisen out of the desire and need to take care of or "guard what has been entrusted to you" (1 Timothy 6:20). The kit *Reducing the Risk of Child Sexual Abuse in Your Church* [4] includes suggestions for procedures and forms to use as you screen individuals. Sample volunteer screening forms can be found in *Sunday School for a New Century* and on *PRESource* at www.lifeway.com/presource.

In addition to screening teachers, you can take other **SAFETY** measures to protect preschoolers.

Security procedures for releasing preschoolers only to authorized adults

Ability to view the entire room through a small window in the classroom door

Follow policies for immediate reporting of any suspected child abuse

Education and supervision of all teachers

Two or more unrelated teachers with each age group of preschoolers at all times
(regardless of the number of children and the size of the church)

You use universal health precautions[5] when changing diapers and assisting in rest rooms

What safety measures has your church taken for preschoolers?

Training Leaders and Teachers

Kent looked over the list of new preschool teachers.

"We've enlisted some excellent teachers," he said to Rose.

"Now we have to help them know how to do the best job."

An effective preschool ministry team can be developed and nurtured through training. Training for teachers of preschoolers is vital for their personal growth and development. The example of Jesus and the disciples is one of the best models for training. Jesus mentored His disciples, and then He sent them out to teach. A division director may choose some adults to cultivate as preschool teachers. These "apprentice" teachers can serve with an experienced teacher as a mentor. They can substitute in a preschool class/department. After a period of mentoring, these apprentices may decide to teach regularly in a preschool class/department.

In addition to the mentor-apprentice training, churches may use other types of training to develop teachers. A church or Preschool Division should consider developing an annual training calendar, scheduling training events well in advance.

- **Independent Study**—Leaders and teachers can use books, study modules, cassette tapes, videos, and other resources to develop skills. *The Christian Growth Study Plan Catalog* lists resources and diploma study options.
  - **Leadership Meetings**—Leadership meetings provide a natural time for leaders and teachers to develop skills in specific areas of Sunday School ministry. Training may occur with all Sunday School leaders and teachers meeting together or targeted to specific needs in age-group division meetings.
  - **Churchwide Training Events**—A church can plan special training events to meet the needs of teachers.
    - One-Day Extravaganzas—Training is offered on a Friday night, Saturday morning, or Saturday afternoon.
    - Quarterly Training—Training is scheduled every quarter, following a detailed training plan for each age group. The events include dinner and the training session.
    - Semi-Annual Training—Special events are planned to develop skills of all church leaders and teachers.
      - **Associational Training Events, State Training Events, National Training Events**—A church can communicate information about training events provided by an association, a state convention, or agencies of the Southern Baptist Convention. Church leaders and teachers may also develop skills at Sunday School Leadership Events at the national conference centers.

Teachers go through developmental stages as they teach. They can be at any stage at any time. It is possible to meet the needs of teachers in the following four stages when a variety of training opportunities are used.

STAGE 1: *Survival*—This stage usually takes place the first year of teaching. Teachers are unsure if they will even make it through the first months, let alone finish out the year. BASICS should be shared during this stage. This is also a good time for mentoring to occur.

STAGE 2: *Consolidation*—By the end of the first year, teachers generally will have made it to this stage. They begin to feel that they are using their gifts, and their confidence is on the rise. Training during this stage would include a review of the basics and participation in the *Christian Growth Study Plan*.

STAGE 3: *Renewal*—About the third or fourth year, teachers tend to lose some of their enthusiasm and motivation. They may have lost their focus or direction. Goal-setting and ministering may be the focus for training during this stage. Teachers will respond to both formal and informal training. Attending training at Ridgecrest Conference Center (North Carolina), Glorieta Conference Center (New Mexico), or Green Lake Conference Center (Wisconsin) can be helpful during this stage as well as other stages.

STAGE 4: *Maturity*—Teachers in this stage probably will have experienced a passion call. They now have become experienced teachers and are willing to mentor others. At this stage, a variety of methods will help meet their training needs.[6]

Pray that God will lead you to someone who needs a mentor.

What training opportunities have you taken advantage of recently?

How do you plan to continue to grow in your knowledge of preschool education?

Personal Bible Study

"Do you enjoy teaching preschoolers?" Pastor Mike asked Maria.

"Yes," Maria said, "but sometimes I miss my Sunday School class. How can I continue to learn about God and the Bible when I'm not in Sunday School with other adults?"

You may be asking the question, "How do I grow spiritually if I am teaching preschoolers?" Meeting the spiritual needs of teachers is extremely important. Personal Bible study is important for teachers to help them be filled spiritually and ready to teach preschoolers from their spiritual overflow. Teachers then are ready for spontaneous teachable moments. The following are suggestions for helping meet some of the spiritual needs of teachers.

- Personal Bible study
- Bible study with other preschool leaders and teachers
- Participation in a Bible study group
- Christian fellowship with other adults
- Inclusion in an Adult Sunday School class through the "in service" roll
- Regular worship attendance

"I am so glad we have so many who are willing to teach preschoolers and minister to them and their families," thought Kent. "I would like to think of a special way to tell the teachers how much we appreciate them."

Teacher appreciation is an important part of any growing ministry. Leaders and teachers need to know that they are valued and that the church recognizes the importance of their ministries. There are several ways to show appreciation to teachers. Simple appreciation ideas include:

- Phone calls—encourage parents, church leaders, and church members to call teachers and express a thanks for teaching preschoolers.
- Prayer lines—place the names of preschool teachers in a prayer room or in a special prayer bulletin insert.
- Appreciation fellowship or banquet
- Personal notes—encourage parents of preschoolers to write a note or letter to their child's preschool teachers.

Consider the following ideas as you "TREAT" others the way you would like to be treated.

Train—Teachers need to be equipped for the very important ministry of teaching preschoolers.

Reward—A small means of recognition is well worth the effort to show teachers how proud we are of them and their accomplishments.

Encourage—Encouragement can be given in many ways—from a simple "WOW!" to a pat on the back, a smile, or bigger events such as Teacher Appreciation Sunday.

Affirm—All teachers need to feel valued.

Thank you—This is a simple phrase, but one that speaks volumes.[7]

Take the time to "TREAT" those with whom you minister. Remember, you do not serve alone.

List several ways you can show appreciation to those who minister with you.

"Who then will teach the children?" The answer is: God-called individuals who are using their gifts and talents to lay foundations in the lives of preschoolers that will last a lifetime.

---

[1] Adapted from *Natural Church Development: A Guide to Eight Essential Qualities of Healthy Churches,* Christian A. Schwarz (Carol Stream, IL: Church Smart Resources, 1996), 24.

[2] Bill L. Taylor, *The Complete Guide for Building a Great Commission Sunday School 1998-99: The Power to Change Lives* (Nashville: Convention Press, 1998), 145.

[3] From the *International Child's Bible Dictionary* (Waco: Word Publishing, 1989), 82.

[4] To order Richard Hammar's book *Reducing the Risk of Sexual Abuse in Your Church,* contact Christian Ministry Resources, P. O. Box 1098. Matthews, NC 28106.

[5] Ibid., Chapter 4 (for more detailed information).

[6] Lillian G. Katz, *Talks with Teachers* (Washington D.C. National Association for the Education of the Young Child, 1977), 7-13.

[7] Used by permission from Dr. John R. "Dick" Lincoln, pastor, Shandon Baptist Church, Columbia, SC.

CHAPTER 5
Connecting Through

Kent knocked on Joe's office door.

"How's the move?" Kent asked.

"We're getting settled in," Joe said. "Moving to a new state has been hard, especially with two kids. Everything is unpacked, and Ashley started kindergarten last week." Joe laughed. "We're making it, even if we do have trouble finding the grocery store sometimes."

As Kent walked back to his own office, he thought, "Could our church do something to help Joe's family?"

A significant part of teaching in a preschool class/department involves ministering to preschoolers and their families, witnessing to parents of preschoolers, and assimilating preschool families into the life of the church through Bible study, worship, and fellowship. The task of working with preschoolers does not begin and end with teaching on Sunday but goes beyond the church door to connect with families during the week.

In Matthew 25:40, Jesus indicates that when Christians minister "unto the least of these," they are, in effect, ministering to Him. Many opportunities to minister become apparent as leaders and teachers seek to involve preschoolers and their families in the church. Ministry can occur in times of great joy, in times of crisis, and in the day-to-day moments of life. Some of the specific times and ways preschool leadership can minister are shown in the following chart:

Illness of a Child
- Help with doctor's visits
- Provide child care for siblings
- Deliver meals

Illness of a Parent
- Prepare meals
- Do grocery shopping
- Offer child care

Birth of a New Baby
- Bring gifts for siblings
- Supply child care for siblings
- Furnish meals

Ministry

Loss of Job
- Arrange financial aid
- Deliver meals or groceries
- Give emotional support

Move of a Family
- Supply information about the community
- Help with child care
- Provide a meal on moving day

Miscarriage
- Offer emotional support
- Deliver meals
- Provide support group

Divorce
- Listen to children's concerns
- Provide emotional support
- Provide support groups

Preschoolers and their families also need support in the day-to-day moments of life. Support for developing families could be provided through:

- parenting seminars and classes,
- parenting resources, and
- mentoring programs.

Can you think of other times and ways you can minister to preschoolers and their families?

Ministering to Children with Special Needs

"I'm so glad the Martins came to church today," commented Brenda.

"I think that they were a little nervous about leaving Joshua," said Maria. "I tried to reassure them that he would be all right. I told them I knew how to use a heart monitor because my oldest child had one when he was a baby."

Families which include children with special needs face all the same challenges as other families, often with greater intensity. Preschool leaders and teachers can minister to these families in many ways, if they are sensitive.

Preschool leaders and teachers can:

- provide child care so that parents can take a day or night off.
- provide help with visits to the doctor or therapist.
- provide training for leaders and teachers to help them understand how to teach and minister to children with special needs.
- provide support groups for parents of children with special needs.
- provide space that meets the needs of children with special needs.

To effectively reach or minister to any family, the church must consider the uniqueness of the family, including special needs and culture.

Ministering to Families from Different Cultures

Many cities have families from different cultural backgrounds. Christ has called the church to go to all the world, but in some cases, the world has come to the church's neighborhood! Churches who want to minister to people of all cultures should look for ways to meet the needs of those families. Some needs may not differ from the needs of any other preschool family. However, the family may have some unique needs. A church who seeks to meet needs of all families will reach families for Christ.

Families who have moved to the United States may be eager to learn English. A church that offers English classes may reach these families. An English class can be an entry to involve a family in other church ministries. A church can encourage its English "students" to return on Sundays for Bible study and worship. Preschoolers may become involved in Sunday School because the church offered to teach English to their parents. Meeting the need of learning English can help a church minister to international families.

A church that seeks to meet the needs of all families will recognize when it may not be the right church for a family. Church leaders can become familiar with international congregations in the area. Churches can partner together to minister to families. When an unchurched family is discovered, a church leader can give the name to the appropriate international church. Occasionally, the churches can worship together. Worshiping with other churches can cultivate an appreciation for the richness of cultural differences.

FIRST CONTACT

"I really would like to teach in Sunday School," said Josie, "but my job as a neonatal nurse requires that I work every other weekend. I really wish I could do something to help on the weeks I don't work."

Kent thought about Josie's words and wondered if there was some way to combine her knowledge of babies and her desire to minister to preschool families.

"I wonder if she would be willing to visit new parents?" Kent asked himself.

FIRST CONTACT is a program of ongoing outreach and ministry to expectant parents and parents of preschoolers up to 12 months old. A preschool staff person, Sunday School director, or Preschool Division director may decide to start a FIRST CONTACT ministry. The Preschool Division outreach-evangelism director, who has the primary responsibility of leading in prospect discovery and visitation assignments, may coordinate the efforts of FIRST CONTACT.

A church can follow these steps to start a FIRST CONTACT program:

1. Begin by enlisting a core group of volunteer visitors. Volunteer visitors may be enlisted to visit one or two families. These visitors may be:
   - adults with a love for young families who are unchurched;
   - couples from Young Adult Sunday School classes;
   - adults active in the church's outreach-evangelism ministry; or
   - Sunday School teachers who have the prospects and family members in Bible study.
2. Communicate the ministry of FIRST CONTACT to the church membership through the church newsletter, leaflets, or bulletin boards. Use these methods to familiarize adults with opportunities to reach young families. As a result, interested adults may volunteer their time for visitation and ministry.
3. Develop a detailed approach to ongoing prospect discovery. Involve the Preschool Division director and all department leadership in locating prospects on a regular basis. Prospect discovery ideas might include:
   - new birth listings in the local newspaper;
   - Vacation Bible School prospects whose siblings are 12 months and younger;
   - names from a newcomers list published by the Chamber of Commerce; or
   - names of prospects given by church members from their workplace or neighborhood.
4. Meet with volunteer visitors on a regular basis (monthly) to review visits made during the month, make new visitation assignments, and make plans for future prospect discovery efforts.
5. Train volunteer visitors to make contacts. Encourage volunteers to develop visiting and witnessing skills. Involve the pastor, minister of education, or outreach director in the training process. Training may coincide with a Sunday School leadership event or during a regular FIRST CONTACT meeting.

6. Budget for resources and supplies needed for visitation, outreach events, and publicity events. The outreach director may prepare a budget for the Preschool Division director.
7. Develop a calendar that includes special events (such as Parent/Child Dedication, prospect discovery events).

contact 1•2•3

"There is so much to remember about being a teacher," thought Maria. "I wish I knew an easy way to keep in contact with the children in my class and the preschool prospects."

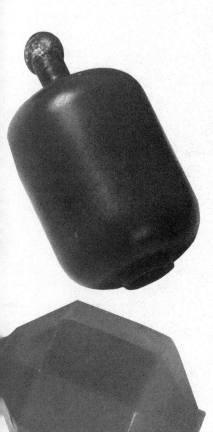

What is contact 1•2•3?
contact 1•2•3 is a plan for encouraging preschool teachers to make ongoing contacts to members and prospects. Each member and prospect is assigned to a preschool leader.

How are assignments made?
- *GEOGRAPHY*—Assignments might be made based on where teachers live.
- *ATTENDANCE PATTERNS*—Assignments might be made based on the regularity of attendance of the preschoolers.
- *MINISTRY NEEDS*—Assignments may be made based on the ministry needs of preschoolers and families. Some families will need more attention; some preschool leaders and teachers are better equipped to meet particular needs.
- Any combination of these factors may serve as the basis for ministry assignments.

*How are contacts made in **contact 1•2•3**?*
- By mail
- By telephone
- Through personal visits

When should contacts be made?
- When a child is absent
- When ministry is indicated
- On special occasions
- On a regular, ongoing basis
- When the church plans special events of interest to families
- When preschool teachers need to communicate information

All preschool teachers can implement **contact 1•2•3**, whatever the class size or church size.

Making Home Visits

Preschool leaders and teachers can acquire valuable insights about preschoolers they teach and their families through home visits. Many leaders and teachers visit in the homes of their preschoolers once a quarter when they deliver literature.

Tips for Making a Home Visit

- Visit in pairs, never alone.
- Phone ahead and make an appointment.
- Keep appropriate materials in the trunk of your car so that you will have what you need for a visit.
- Keep visits short.

Materials to use for a home visit might include:

- current Sunday School materials for parents and children,
- parenting or family magazines, and
- materials for simple art projects to complete with a child.

> "Come in," Joe said to Kent and his friends.
> "We are glad your family came to our church," Kent said.
> Joe smiled. "Thanks," he said. "We enjoyed it."
> Kent gestured to his friends. "Mark and Sarah have been coming to our church for several months. In fact, if you came to Sunday School, you would be in the same class as Mark and Sarah. Mark, why don't you tell Joe about Sunday School?"

When ministering to preschool families, leaders and teachers must be sensitive to the leading of the Holy Spirit to share their faith with unsaved parents. Each person's greatest need is salvation through Jesus Christ. Jesus can change the lives of parents and, through their influence, the lives of preschoolers.

A preschool teacher may be the tool that God chooses to use to reach parents. A teacher has regular, ongoing contact with the family. As the teacher builds a relationship with parents, she may have an opportunity to talk about her own journey of faith in Jesus. Teachers can share their personal testimonies and use Scriptures to help guide parents to a better understanding of the gospel message.

One plan to help the Sunday School impact families with the gospel is FAITH: Sunday School Evangelism Strategy. FAITH is an evangelism strategy linked directly to the Sunday School. FAITH teams are comprised of adults who attend the same Sunday School class or department. Preschool teachers may be assigned to teams with members of the preschool parents' Sunday School department.

Teams visit prospects and members of their department or class. Sometimes teams visit preschoolers or family members who need care or ministry. The team can discover needs and report the needs to the class/department. After the visit, teachers can plan how to minister to the child or family. Sometimes teams visit

families who are prospects. The team can witness to unsaved parents and communicate the opportunities for Bible study for the entire family. In leadership planning meetings, teachers can plan ways to follow up visits by the FAITH teams.

Preschool teachers not directly involved in the FAITH ministry can help through support of FAITH. Teachers can pray regularly for members of the FAITH teams and for preschool families who are church members and prospects. Teachers can acquire all pertinent information about any family that visits in the preschool classes/departments and make sure that the information is referred to the FAITH ministry through the division outreach/evangelism director. Teachers can report any care or ministry needs of a family so that a FAITH team can visit. Sunday School and FAITH work together to minister to families and reach families with Christ's love.

Fellowship

Brenda and Maria walked together to the parking lot.

"That was a fun morning," Brenda said. "I'm glad you are teaching with me."

"It's fun!" Maria said.

Maria saw some parents talking together.

"I wish we could get all of our parents together," Maria said, "you know, for fun and to talk. I'm sure they could help each other."

Preschoolers and their families need to feel welcomed and accepted—to feel that they belong and are part of the group. Preschool leaders and teachers help foster that belonging through fellowship. Fellowship involves developing warm relationships and drawing others into those relationships.

Much of what a teacher does during Sunday School helps develop these relationships. By planning and preparing, greeting preschoolers, and providing appropriate Bible-learning experiences, teachers develop warm relationships with preschoolers. By ministering to families and meeting needs, a teacher also develops relationships with the families.

Sometimes fellowship is a spontaneous event. A teacher may invite families to lunch. Families may go together to an ice-cream shop after church on Sunday night. Sometimes fellowship is more planned and deliberate. Leaders and teachers can plan special events for families to fellowship together. A fellowship event may include celebrating family triumphs, recognizing personal successes, welcoming a new baby, or gathering for an old-fashioned party for preschoolers and parents.

Keep these tips in mind when planning family fellowships:
- Plan events that do not conflict with other church events. Avoid holidays and major church emphases (such as a revival).
- Plan events that the whole family can attend.

- Enlist others to help organize the fellowship (decorations, food, games, publicity).
- Publicize the event early (about two months before the event). Use signs, newsletters, flyers, notes, and other means to inform families of the fellowship.
- Make sure that all games, food, and other items are safe for preschoolers.
- Allow time for families to mingle and talk. Do not overstructure the event.
- Be prepared for the unexpected, such as rain. Bring a first-aid kit to the event.

Plan fellowships for all times of the year. Here is one idea for each season:

Fall—Leaf Day
Dress: wear fall colors
Decorations: fall leaves
Food: hot cocoa, leaf-shaped cookies
Games: leaf painting, leaf through books, rake leaves

Winter—Indoor Beach Party
Dress: casual clothes
Decorations: beach towels, beach umbrellas, shells
Food: picnic foods
Games: beach ball toss, ball games, tubs of sand for sand castles

Spring—Teddy Bear Picnic
Dress: comfortable clothes
Decorations: teddy bears, blankets
Food: Teddy Grahams, gingerbread bears, Gummi Bears
Games: anything with teddy bears can be used (relays, dress up, 3-legged races)

Summer—"Cool Off" Carnival
Dress: casual, summertime clothes
Decorations: winter items, paper snowflakes
Food: snowball cupcakes, snow cones
Games: mitten relay, winter clothes relay, shaved ice in a tub with sand toys

Use fellowship events to discover prospects. Invite prospects and church visitors to all church events. Encourage families to bring friends. At a fellowship event, register all families who attend (even members). Provide something for families to take home as they leave the fellowship. Include church's name, address, and phone number on anything sent home. After the event, add names of prospects to the prospect file.

Any activity planned by a church represents an opportunity to identify and reach prospects. Other examples might include:

- Vacation Bible School,
- Mother's Day Out,
- parents night out,
- day camp, and
- churchwide picnic.

Make sure that the names of any prospects discovered are added to the prospect file and assigned to a class/department for regular contact.

Worship

Worship includes experiences designed to help persons sense God's presence and respond in praise and adoration. Worship may be individual or corporate. Preschool teachers can guide preschoolers to begin to express praise and thanks to God and to worship God in individual experiences. Teachers can provide appropriate Bible-learning centers/activities that encourage children to experience God and respond to Him at their levels of understanding and ability. Usually a child will experience awe and wonder at God through His creation. As a preschooler smells a flower, tastes an apple, feels a rough rock, hears a bird's song, and sees colorful leaves, he can think about God and the things God made. He can pray, "Thank You, God, for flowers."

He may sing a song about God making apples and other good food. He can hear a Bible verse about God. He can worship God in simple, spontaneous ways.

Worship experiences are also corporate. Congregations gather weekly to worship God. Fours through kindergartners can be a part of this worship time. Parents and other adults can help preschoolers participate in corporate worship experiences and can guide their children to learn more about worshiping God with others. Parents may feel uneasy about taking a child to a worship service. These guidelines can help adults prepare their children for attending worship services:

- Tour the worship center with the child when it is empty. Sit in a pew. Look at a hymnal, a Bible, and any other materials in the pew racks. Walk around the front of the church. Look at the pulpit and the choir loft. A child will ask fewer questions if he is familiar with the worship center.
- Talk with the child about what will happen during worship. Use simple, concrete language. If she knows generally what will occur, a preschooler may ask fewer questions during the service.
- Arrange for the child to talk with someone who helps during a worship service. A choir member, an usher, the pastor, or an instrumentalist can talk with your child about his part of the service.
- Before worship, allow the child to go to the rest room and water fountain. Some children enjoy a short walk outside before entering the worship center. (A walk can release energy and prepare the child for a period of sitting.)
- Enter the worship center calmly and unhurriedly, to set a worshipful mood.
- Choose a seat so that the child can see (near the front, at the end of a pew).
- Allow the child to move. She will not be able to sit perfectly still during the entire worship experience. (Adults do not sit still; they wiggle, too.)
- Encourage the child to participate in worship. He can stand when others stand, hold open a hymnal or Bible, put money in the offering plate, or sing a chorus.
- Answer any questions the child asks. Do not ignore her or she may talk louder to get your attention. Before attending worship, practice using a quiet voice.
- After worship, discuss what happened. Compliment your child on his positive behavior.

Helping preschoolers learn to worship, telling parents about Jesus, building warm relationships with families, and meeting needs of people are all important aspects of a total preschool ministry. By ministering to preschoolers and their families, leaders and teachers help people understand the relevance of Jesus in the world today. Teachers help connect the Bible to those living in a new century.

CHAPTER 6
Connecting Through

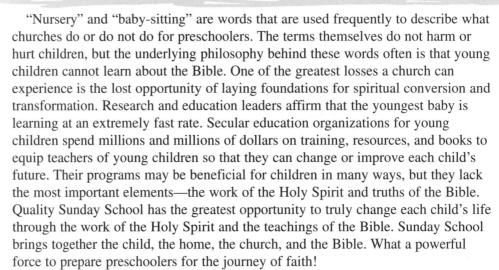

Carmen's mother looked in the Sunday School room.
"That doesn't look like Sunday School," she said to Maria. "They are not sitting and listening. It looks like all they are doing is playing. How are they going to learn about the Bible if they are playing?"

"Nursery" and "baby-sitting" are words that are used frequently to describe what churches do or do not do for preschoolers. The terms themselves do not harm or hurt children, but the underlying philosophy behind these words often is that young children cannot learn about the Bible. One of the greatest losses a church can experience is the lost opportunity of laying foundations for spiritual conversion and transformation. Research and education leaders affirm that the youngest baby is learning at an extremely fast rate. Secular education organizations for young children spend millions and millions of dollars on training, resources, and books to equip teachers of young children so that they can change or improve each child's future. Their programs may be beneficial for children in many ways, but they lack the most important elements—the work of the Holy Spirit and truths of the Bible. Quality Sunday School has the greatest opportunity to truly change each child's life through the work of the Holy Spirit and the teachings of the Bible. Sunday School brings together the child, the home, the church, and the Bible. What a powerful force to prepare preschoolers for the journey of faith!

The goal of Sunday School is to lay foundations that will lead to spiritual conversion and lifelong spiritual transformation. Spiritual transformation is God's work of changing a believer into the likeness of Jesus by creating a new identity in Christ and by empowering a lifelong relationship of love, trust, and obedience to glorify God.[1] Spiritual conversion is the first step in spiritual transformation. The journey toward spiritual conversion should begin in the arms of parents and Sunday School teachers. When adults choose moments to point the child to God by saying, "Thank You, God, for Katie," they are beginning the journey.

A child's worldview is being shaped from the first days of life. The child is born asking: "Who am I?" "Why am I here?" "Where do I fit in?" These questions are too important to be left to day-care centers, schools, peers, or church baby-sitting. Parents and teachers begin to answer these questions through experiences with the Bible. They can begin to use the Bible with babies. Looking at pictures and turning pages allow a baby to have hands-on experiences with the Bible. As the child grows older, he can touch a word, find a Bible verse marker, and read a verse. Choosing to use the same or similar Bible at home and church allows the child to identify this important book in both places. As a preschooler grows

Teaching

older, he can see the personal Bibles of parents and teachers. He will "catch" attitudes regarding the Bible, attitudes of his parents and teachers. His feelings and attitudes will be strengthened by repeatedly hearing words like *love, Jesus, Bible,* and *God* in association with interesting and challenging activities. These associations create strong connections in the heart, mind, and soul of a child.

The home is the first and central place of Bible teaching. The impact of Sunday School is limited without the connection with the home. A church may provide excellent Bible-learning experiences but miss the mark in connecting with parents. For foundational Bible teaching to make life impact, teachers and leaders must focus on the parents as well as the children. The average child spends 35 to 40 hours a week in front of a television screen or video game. Most preschoolers and children are spending more time with media in one week than they spend with the life-changing message of the Bible in a year. The only way to change this statistic is by focusing on the home as the primary place for Bible teaching. This is not a new idea. Moses described this principle in Deuteronomy 6:6-7: "These commandments I give to you today are to be upon your hearts. Impress them on your children. Talk about them when you sit at home and when you walk along the road, when you lie down and when you get up." Parents should incorporate teaching the Bible as a habit, a practice, and a lifestyle.

"I do not think that real Bible teaching can occur outside the context of relationships."

- O. Eugene Mims

Ways Preschoolers Learn

As parents and teachers teach preschoolers biblical truths, they should keep in mind eight basic ways all preschoolers learn. While preschoolers are unique and grow through stages at different rates, these eight basic ways preschoolers learn remain constant. Each teaching moment, regardless of the age or stage of a preschooler, should address at least one of these avenues.

Senses—Preschoolers learn to discover the things God has made through touching, smelling, tasting, hearing, and seeing. A valuable learning experience allows preschoolers to use their hands, eyes, noses, ears, and mouths as a part of the learning process. Teachers of preschoolers often focus their teaching activities only around seeing and hearing. However, involving more senses causes the learning experience to become more real. Teaching that involves the senses requires more preparation and resources, but its impact will make learning more memorable.

Curiosity—Exploring the world is a lifelong process. Curiosity in the adult world is evidenced by the space programs, science, technology, archaeology, and through many careers and fields of study. A preschooler's curiosity drives him to explore, discover, and ask the question "why?" Teachers and parents

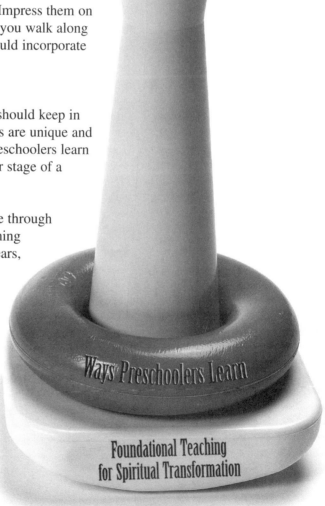

should facilitate exploration, providing an interesting and stimulating environment. Adults can shape the child's worldview by connecting explorations and discoveries to God, the Creator and Sustainer of life.

Hands-On Experience—Today the term "hands-on" is used to describe anything that involves a child doing something. This definition leads to the misconception that keeping a child busy and involved is the end, or goal, of teaching. "Hands-on" truly means involving the child in an activity that leads her to a greater understanding of a Bible truth. In hands-on teaching, preschoolers are guided through an activity toward a Bible truth that can be understood and applied in that moment and in the child's life. Hands-on teaching provides concrete experiences with Bible truths.

Relationships form the eternal connnections between the child and biblical truth.

Satisfaction—Should Sunday School be "satisfaction guaranteed"? When a child is involved in satisfying experiences, he gains a sense of accomplishment. Through this sense of accomplishment, the child can realize that he is unique and created in the image of God. Satisfaction affirms the individual's importance to God and his dependence on God for all good gifts. A satisfying environment gives the child choices that allow him to learn in the ways God has gifted him.

Relationships—Relationships form the eternal connections between the child and the biblical truth. To understand the message of the Bible, adults use various translations, commentaries, and Bible dictionaries. For preschoolers, who do not have the benefit of adult language, the relationship with a teacher becomes a living commentary on the Scripture. Parents and teachers represent God, His Word, and His Power as they relate to preschoolers. Moses used the words "impress it upon their hearts" (Deuteronomy 6:7). Adults "impress" God's love and truth in preschoolers' lives through warm, caring relationships.

Imitation—How does a child learn to respect and love others? She begins to learn by the way she is loved and respected. Preschoolers follow the lead of adults in their lives. Actions as well as words of adults teach the child. Long before a baby can understand the words of adults, she understands their actions. Preschoolers learn to follow Christ's example by following paths adults choose.

Play—Playing and learning are inseparable for preschoolers. Play offers the greatest opportunity for Bible teaching. Through play, a child can learn and apply important truths, relate in positive ways to others, accept responsibility, and solve problems. But play is just activity unless the teacher guides the activity and discussion toward foundational biblical truths.

Repetition—"Not this Bible story again." This statement is uttered by some adults who teach preschoolers. However, preschoolers need the repetition of Bible truths and Bible stories. The use of repetition allows preschoolers to gain more knowledge and application of the truths. The children begin to feel more confident about the Bible story. As children grow, their knowledge and understanding grow. Repetition allows the child to build on previous foundational truths and understand more fully the truths he has already heard.

Individual Approaches to Learning

Understanding the general ways preschoolers learn is essential, but it is only the first step to understanding how to teach preschoolers. Preschoolers are born with certain characteristics, and they develop other personality traits. As they grow, girls and boys also develop individual approaches to learning. The biblical evidences of these varied approaches to learning are reflected throughout Jesus' life and teachings. Jesus knew that the individuals He discipled learned in distinctive ways. He used a diversity of approaches during the same teaching situation to meet the individual needs of His learners. Jesus realized that God created people with different ways of learning and dealing with life situations.

As Jesus did, a preschool teacher must provide a learning environment that addresses the differences in learners. The role of the teacher is to create an environment and guide learning in ways that will facilitate the work of the Holy Spirit and to provide foundational teaching that will eventually lead to spiritual conversion and transformation. A teacher must recognize the varied ways preschoolers approach learning and their individual levels of learning. To ensure that all learners encounter the message, a teacher must use methods that incorporate several approaches. A teacher should evaluate how well she achieves life impact of specific lessons, especially the spiritual-transformation goals of laying foundations.

A foundational element of any approach to learning or teaching is the role of the Bible story. The stories of God's redemptive work form the core of all learning that leads to foundational teaching and spiritual transformation. The biblical tradition of telling the stories of God's work to generation after generation forms the beginning threads of the Old Testament. This oral tradition can be found today in preschool classes/departments, in churches, and in homes everywhere. Whether dressing up and playing out a Bible story, hearing a book about a Bible person, creating a picture while hearing facts about a Bible family, or saying a thank-you prayer to God while tasting oranges, the story—God's story—is the content that prepares and changes lives.

While God created every preschooler to be unique, preschoolers of all ages approach learning in one or more of the following ways: relational, musical, logical, natural, physical, reflective, visual, and verbal. While every adult has dominant approaches to learning, she can learn through multiple approaches, often simultaneously. During the preschool years, dominant approaches may be difficult to distinguish; therefore, a teacher must provide a variety of approaches during a session to meet the variety of needs and approaches. Dominant approaches also may change as preschoolers move through different life stages. By providing a variety of approaches to learn the same Bible truths, teachers will be guiding preschoolers to learn in the ways God created them to learn.

Relational

These preschoolers are highly social, make friends easily, and may be very good talkers. They are keen observers of other children and adults, noticing their moods and motivations. Recognizing how people feel enables relational children to respond accordingly. They are drawn to activities that allow them to cooperate and interact with others. This approach naturally includes homeliving activities but also includes any activity that involves group interaction. These children may become known as "people persons."

Worldview is a frame of reference that defines the way a person thinks and acts.

Musical
Most preschoolers enjoy musical experiences. Some preschoolers from birth seem more sensitive to rhythm and pitch than others. They tend to be good listeners. Because they are more comfortable with music, singing and movement are their natural responses to music. These preschoolers may learn new songs quickly and remember them easily. They find it easy to express themselves through music—making up their own songs, playing instruments, and performing for others.

Logical
Problem solving is an enjoyable experience for some preschoolers. They see patterns in the world and can reason through difficult situations. They enjoy games and puzzles. They quickly understand the concepts of "less than" and "same as." These children will want step-by-step explanations with details. These learners, as older preschoolers, may enjoy brain teasers or problem-solving games.

Natural
These preschoolers enjoy the beauty of God's creation. They can easily learn to identify the elements of the natural world. They may relate well to stories in the Bible that allude to elements in nature. Investigation and exploration of God's world are appealing to these preschoolers. They have a fascination for plants and animals and a high sensitivity for taking care of God's world.

Physical
Preschoolers who approach learning from a physical standpoint are very active and may have good coordination. When telling a story, they not only use words, they play it out. Physical learners also may be inclined to learn through mission projects or other helping activities. They use their physical abilities and skills in games and dramas. They use their entire bodies.

Reflective
Reflective learners tend to understand who they are and how they feel. Working alone may be their desire. Preschoolers who utilize this approach to learning do not shun the company of children but often choose activities that allow self-expression. These preschoolers are comfortable with extended periods of solitude. They may internalize concepts by personalizing them.

Visual
Visual learners can "see" in their imaginations as well as in the concrete world. They also enjoy creating their own pictures and visual representations of what they are learning. Interacting with teaching pictures is a preferred experience for these preschoolers. They hear stories and visualize the events through word pictures. Visual learners are not necessarily drawn to creating art.

Verbal
Some preschoolers learn best through words—reading (or being read to), writing (or dictating), speaking, and listening. Verbal learners like the sounds of words and may have large vocabularies. Preschoolers with this approach to learning like to talk and play word games. They enjoy stories, poems, and jokes.

Remember that preschoolers will operate out of several approaches in varying degrees. By observing children in the class or during a home visit, teachers can plan teaching activities that lead to spiritual transformation.

Read the description of each biblical personality.
Choose an approach to learning that the personality illustrates.

BIBLE CHARACTERS

____ In Acts, Joseph of Cyprus was soon renamed Barnabas ("the encourager") because of the way he related to the church, its ministry, and to other Christians. He was an advocate for Paul and John Mark.

____ When making a point to his readers, Paul often used a very logical argument or formal debate style. He stated evidence from the Old Testament. He appealed to logic and reason in matters of grace and faith. The Book of Romans is an example of approaching learning and teaching through logic.

____ As David penned his psalms, he expressed his faith in musical form. His words form the basis for many contemporary choruses and hymns of praise.

____ Ezekiel has been described as an ecstatic kind of prophet. His unique approach to "forth telling" and "fore-telling" drew great attention during his ministry. He acted out many of his prophesies to make points that were memorable in the minds and lives of his contemporaries.

____ Many of the psalms approach teaching and learning from a sensitivity to the natural world. Psalms 8, 23, and 139 are all examples of David's experience with God and His mighty works. David saw God active in nature all around him.

____ Solomon's writings are an example of an individual who approached learning from a verbal perspective. His speech at the dedication of the temple in 1 Kings 8 demonstrates a verbal approach to learning and teaching.

____ During the significant times in the life of Mary, the Gospels portray her as a woman who pondered God's will and her role in His plan. She found times of reflection to be her own personal teachable moments.

____ John, as he wrote the Gospel, epistles, and Revelation, used vivid images to paint pictures for his readers. Light and darkness were just two elements John used to teach his followers about God and godliness.

APPROACHES TO LEARNING

A. Natural

B. Visual

C. Relational

D. Physical

E. Reflective

F. Musical

G. Verbal

H. Logical

RESOURCES RELATED TO APPROACHES TO LEARNING

Armstrong, Thomas. *Seven Kinds of Smart.* Plume Book, New York City, New York, 1993.

LeFever, Marlene D. *Learning Styles: Reaching Everyone God Gave You to Teach.* David C. Cook Publishing Co., Colorodo Springs, Colorado, 1995.

Gardner, Howard. *Multiple Intelligences.* Basic Books, 1993.

Tobias, Cynthia. *Every Child Can Succeed.* Focus on the Family Publishing, Colorado Springs, Colorado, 1996.

Tobias, Cynthia. *The Way They Learn.* Focus on the Family Publishing, Colorado Springs, Colorado, 1996.

Wiley, R. Scott. "All Roads Lead to Learning," *Preschool Bible Teacher C,* Winter 1997-98.

> Bible-learning centers/activities should occur simultaneously to allow preschoolers freedom of choice and freedom to move.

> **BONUS IDEA:** Use short-sleeved men's shirts for child-sized paint smocks. Open a portion of the sleeve hem, insert a 7-inch length of soft elastic, and stitch the ends together.

Bible Learning Centers/Activities

In a preschool committee meeting, members talked about assembling a resource room.

"Kent," one asked, "what should be included in that room?"

"The resources should help teachers teach Bible truths," Kent responded. "The resources should be available for Bible-teaching activities."

"What kinds of activities will the teachers use?" asked the committee member.

Knowing about the general ways of learning and individual approaches to learning is the first step in planning an effective Bible-teaching session. Putting the knowledge to work means choosing methods that speak to both the general ways preschoolers learn and the individual approaches to learning. These methods may be grouped around the Bible-learning centers/activities. Preschoolers should be able to move freely to choose among appropriate activities. By making choices, each child will learn in the specific way God gifted him and will be involved in activities that increase the potential of integrating the Bible truths to his life.

Homeliving/Dramatic Play—Provide plastic dishes and soft plastic dolls. Provide two dolls to encourage working together. Use dolls with molded bodies and painted hair and eyes so that the dolls can be disinfected after each session. Add special

items which relate to the Bible story or Bible truth. Preschoolers may enjoy making play dough or food. (Avoid using the same batch of play dough over a long period of time. Germs may be passed from one child to another over the course of time.)

Art/Creative Art—Provide a variety of materials for preschoolers to use creatively. The process of creating and using his own ideas is more important to a child than the final product. The process of creating is eternal while the product that will be lost or discarded in a few hours or days is temporary. What the child takes home in his head and heart will make the difference.

Puzzles/Manipulatives—Provide only three or four wooden puzzles, floor puzzles, or other types of manipulatives that are suited to the age group you teach. (Ones—Twos: 2-6 pieces; Threes—Pre-Kindergarten: 10-20 pieces; Kindergarten: 20-30 pieces) In younger age groups, consider materials for matching, sorting, sequencing, threading, or stringing as the activities relate to the Bible truth. Always use puzzles that have real-life illustrations rather than cartoons.

Nature/Science—Select fresh nature items from your locale which will help reinforce the foundational truths from the Bible. Supervise carefully the use of nature items and consider children's allergies.

Blocks/Construction—Provide cardboard blocks for ones and twos; offer wooden unit blocks for threes and older. Use teaching pictures, transportation toys, stand-up figures, animals, and other building materials. Limit the number of children to three or four at a time. Place this Bible-learning center/activity out of high traffic areas.

Toys—In younger preschool classes/departments, teachers may use toys to invite the child to talk about the Bible story or truth. Select toys that are suitable for the age, durable, washable, and safe.

Books—Use books in the room with any or all Bible-learning centers/activities. For a session, choose four or five books that depict present-day stories and relate to the Bible story. Change books every session to provide variety and spark interest.

Music—Include music throughout the session to give instructions, encourage worship, and teach Bible truths. Music activities can take place in any center and during group time. Music is often a great way to transition to group time or to welcome children to the room.

Take a few moments to think of Bible-learning centers/activities and the preschoolers you teach. Using the space beside the Bible-learning centers/activities below, describe an activity. Then identify the general way preschoolers learn through this method and the individual learning approach that it may address.

TEACHING TIP: Telling the story without "props" allows the children to focus on the words of the story and listen more intently. Preschoolers can use items like child made puppets or flocked-backed figures and a flannel board to recall the Bible story.

BIBLE LEARNING CENTER	ACTIVITY	LEARNING APPROACHES
Homeliving/Dramatic Play	dress up as Moses	physical
Blocks/Construction		
Puzzles/Manipulatives		
Art/Creative Art		
Nature/Science		

Preschoolers today are overwhelmed by media influences including television programs, video cassette tapes, and computer games. These technological marvels have improved our lives in many ways, but they may not be the best choice for a teaching activity. Evaluate these avenues for Bible teaching. Does the medium matter? Can the message be delivered intact and clearly understood to the audience regardless of the medium? Here are some factors to consider about these technologies, especially videos and television:

1. What is the purpose of your session, to educate or entertain? Just because a medium catches a child's focus does not mean he understands the concepts. Listening is not necessarily learning.

2. Does the medium use fantasy characters or cartoons to communicate the Bible truth? Children read many books and hear many stories during the first years of life. They often have difficulty discriminating between fantasy and fact or fantasy and faith. It is essential that you use methods or media that communicate the difference between true Bible stories and animated classics. Through these Bible stories comes the power to transform lives.

3. Does the medium use analogies to communicate Bible truths? Preschoolers are concrete thinkers; it is difficult for them to see the relationship or comparison between otherwise unrelated objects or ideas.

Another activity commonly used with preschoolers is a coloring sheet. Review "The Seven Super Reasons Teachers Use Coloring Sheets to Teach Bible Truths."

1. They are quick. I do not have to gather all those art supplies for preschoolers to use creatively.

2. Parents love them. Parents often comment on how their child colors better than others on the same picture. If children were just drawing or painting on blank paper, parents could not tell which child colored the best.

3. Children need to learn to color in the lines. Who cares about each child's personality? Children need to color fire trucks red and bluebirds blue and stop scribbling.

4. Parents need something to hang on the refrigerator. It does not matter if we get to those Bible phrases, as long as the child has a picture to take home.

5. Preschoolers love cartoons, even if they do not look much like the real people in the Bible.

6. I love it when all the preschoolers have the same thing to take home. Rarely does a child cry because his does not look as good as little Bobbie Dean's (the head deacon's son).

7. My mother used coloring sheets in her department.

This list is for fun and not to be taken seriously. Are coloring sheets the best choice for preschoolers? Coloring sheets often limit a child's feeling of success and short-circuit his own personal interests and gifts. Coloring sheets limit a child's creativity. Coloring sheets also focus on a product which is not eternal. The eternal process occurs when prepared teachers open their hearts and Bibles to young children. Bible learning is greatly impacted when teachers follow Jesus' example of teaching individuals where they are and moving them toward spiritual conversion and transformation. Here are some things to remember:

- Coloring sheets are not realistic. They often are cartoons or stereotypes.
- Coloring sheets do not allow an adequate number of choices to foster creativity.
- Coloring sheets limit a child's ability to choose and to gain satisfaction.

Making Choices for the Learning Environment

Maria looked around her room. "The leader guide suggests all these centers," Maria said to Brenda, "but we only have one table."

"And I don't think there is money to buy more tables," Brenda said.

Knowing what you need most when you are teaching in a small room or with limited resources can be a challenging task. Consider these guidelines:

Sacrifice tables and chairs. Remove chairs and tables to provide space for movement and Bible teaching. Preschoolers can sit on the floor or stand at a table to work. When using a table, push it near the wall to create more space.

Sacrifice storage cabinets. Find other locations for storage or establish a central location for preschool supplies outside the room.

Sacrifice equipment. If you do not have homeliving furniture or shelves, think about using boxes of various sizes. A large shoe box could become a baby bed. An appliance box could become a refrigerator or sink. When space is a premium, remove any large items that are not used meaningfully during the session.

Do not sacrifice the number of teachers. There should always be two teachers in each class/department. This practice provides security for preschoolers, parents, and teachers. Even if some age groups must be combined or you must ask a parent to stay, two adults should be in a preschool room at all times.

Do not sacrifice the teacher/child ratio. Remember that you may not be able to control the amount of space you are given or the resources available, but the number of teachers in the class/department can be controlled. Remember these ratios: Babies, 1:2; Ones and Twos, 1:3; Threes—Pre-K, 1:4; Kindergarten, 1:5; Babies—Twos, 1:3; Threes—Kindergarten, 1:4, Babies—Kindergarten, 1:3.

Do not sacrifice the Leader Guides or Leader Packs. These important resources will help teachers provide appropriate learning activities and experiences for preschoolers. Teachers may find it challenging to plan a cohesive Bible-teaching experience without these resources.

Do not sacrifice the Learner Guides. These resources help carry Bible teaching into homes. Parents can use these take-home materials to guide their children to continue learning Bible truths throughout the week. Learning about God is a continual process, not a Sunday-only event.

Teaching for Spiritual Transformation
Teaching in a manner that leads to conversion and spiritual transformation is not a formula. The Holy Spirit works with each individual in a variety of ways during the course of life. In the lives of preschoolers and young elementary children, the Holy Spirit prepares the way for conversion and spiritual transformation through foundational teaching at home and church. There are seven common elements that may be identified for preschoolers through adults. In older age groups (youth and adults), these elements may be specific and apparent in each session. But for preschoolers, all of these elements may only be seen over the course of time. A few of the elements may not be visible until later in life. These elements are most effective when Sunday School teachers and parents incorporate Bible teaching all week long, providing seven-day-a-week Sunday School.

Acknowledge Authority—Before the session, teachers should prepare for Bible teaching through their personal Bible

Each session has three strategic steps for the teacher.

PREPARE
Teachers prepare through personal encounter with the Bible passage, by gathering the needed resources, and by preparing the room for teaching.

ENCOUNTER
During the session, teachers guide preschoolers to encounter the Bible story and truth through Bible-learning centers/activities and through group time.

CONTINUE
Teachers continue Bible teaching throughout the week by following up with preschoolers and equipping parents to teach Bible truths at home.

study. While preparing for the session, they should seek to understand the influences (or authority) on each child's life. Understanding the home situation, physical condition, and developmental stage of each child will assist the teacher in preparing a teaching plan that focuses the Bible truth in ways that will lead to lifelong learning.

Search the Truth—During the session, teachers should tell the Bible story as it relates to every small group and large group activity. They should open the Bible to the Bible phrases and guide discussion with preschoolers about those Bible phrases. From the first moments to the last moment, preschool teachers should focus on the Scripture.

Discover the Truth—In conversation with preschoolers and in group time, teachers should attempt to explain biblical elements repeatedly throughout the session. Teachers of preschoolers become living commentaries on the passage. Placing Bible stories and concepts in terms a child can understand will assist him in integrating the truth into his life and will lay foundations for future growth.

Personalize the Truth—As preschoolers interact with the Bible-learning centers/activities, they can begin to personalize or integrate the truth into their lives. For Bible truths to be remembered and acted on, they must be useful. Concepts that are not useful will not be remembered or acted on during the immediate context or in future situations.

Struggle with the Truth—At some point, preschoolers will be challenged to think new thoughts. They will encounter new truths. At this point teachers must be willing to address issues and answer questions: "Do you mean that Noah was a real person?" "How did Jesus make people well?" Teachers can support a child's growing understanding of the truths of the Bible by answering questions. Some questions may not have easy answers and may merit the honest response "I don't know that answer." Remember these points about answering questions:

- Do not answer more than a child asks. A child will ask more questions if she needs more information.

- Do not jump to conclusions. Ask follow-up questions to clarify before answering: "What makes you ask that question?" "Tell me more about your question."

- Do not use adult analogies to explain concepts. Speak in clear terms that a child can understand. Preschoolers are learning at very fast rates, but they do not possess an adult's reasoning capabilities.

Believe the Truth—At specific points in time and over a period of time, teachers and parents will have opportunities to shape a child's worldview and belief system. The child will integrate truths into his foundation of faith. Each truth is important, moving toward the day when conversion and spiritual transformation occur. This shaping occurs over a period of time with preschoolers. It is a process of reinforcement at home and church.

Obey the Truth—In some instances, preschoolers will be able to act on a biblical truth. It will shape not only their worldview but their actions. The actions or changes in attitudes will be seen in relation to others as well as relation to God. Obeying the truth is not something the child does in response to adult prodding or rewarding, but is an outward response to an inward change.

"Mrs. Maria," called Enrique's dad. "Thank you for teaching Enrique each Sunday. Last night I picked up our Bible to tell a story to the family. Enrique said, 'Bible!' He is not even two years old yet, and he recognized the Bible."

As the man walked away, Maria prayed, "Thank You, God, for letting me teach preschoolers about You."

• • •

"Kent," Rose said, "Mrs. Fitzgerald just called me. She said their children have enjoyed Sunday School so much. That is one of the main reasons they joined our church."

"I'm glad," Kent said.

Rose continued, "Mrs. Fitzgerald wanted to thank the teachers of four-year-olds. Her daughter has been busy helping all week. Once, Mrs. Fitzgerald heard her say, 'The Bible tells us to help one another.'"

"I'll call and thank the teachers," Kent said. "I'm glad we can minister to preschool families."

It is important for preschool teachers to realize their role in foundational teaching for conversion and spiritual transformation. Attempting to measure every session or unit on outward results will lead to discouragement or pushing preschoolers beyond the work of the Holy Spirit. Remember, the Holy Spirit causes lasting learning which is an eternal change in belief, attitude, and action. Teachers prepare the environment and guide learning to allow the Holy Spirit to work in the lives of learners.

---
[1] Definition of spiritual transformation provided by the Discipleship and Family Ministry Group of the LifeWay Church Resouces Division.

Preschool Resource Management
APPENDIX

Guidelines for obtaining, organizing, and maintaining preschool resources.

Determine What Resources Are Needed
Consult each leader's guide for a list of:
- foundational resources such as a Bible, curriculum, and audio cassette tape.
- basic resources such as toys, books, puzzles, manipulatives, music, blocks, nature, homeliving, and art items.
- specific resources suggested in each session plan

Devise a Plan for Obtaining Resources
- Budget for resources. A preschool council, division director, or staff member should determine an amount adequate for replenishing and maintaining current resources and acquiring new resources.
- A preschool shower can be held. Publicize needs so that individuals or adult departments can purchase items.
- Publish a "wanted" list of household discards and provide a convenient place for collecting donations.

Decide Which Resources Each Department Will Need
Each class/department will need foundational resources (Bible, curriculum) as well as the following basic items:
1. art supplies (for twos and older) assorted paper, crayons, washable felt-tip markers, scissors, non-toxic washable glue, hole punch, and stapler;
2. blocks, toy cars and trucks;
3. books (age suitable and related to subjects God, Jesus, Bible, church, others, family, self, and God's creation);
4. doll (Broadman or other plastic doll with molded hair and features);
5. homeliving items such as toy dishes and toy telephones;
6. hygiene supplies (antibacterial soap, tissues, disinfectant, and diaper-changing supplies);
7. masking tape;
8. play dough, cookie cutters, and rolling pins (for twos and older);
9. puzzles (wooden-inlay puzzles and floor puzzles related to the subjects listed in #3); and
10. toys (for babies, ones, and twos).

Designate a Preschool Resource Room
Look for a central location where supplies can be easily inventoried, maintained, and made available to teachers.
- Enlist a volunteer to maintain or staff the room.
- Schedule a workday when preschool teachers can clean, repair, and organize resources.
- Recruit individuals to sew doll clothes, make smocks for baby rooms, build preschool furniture, cut out magazine pictures and assemble teacher-made toys, games, and puzzles.

- Use storage containers such as:
  - plastic crates, baskets, or dishpans
  - transparent storage boxes with lids
  - shoe boxes, produce boxes, or detergent boxes
  - zip-lock bags in all sizes
  - clear plastic containers (from a deli)
  - empty coffee cans with lids
  - photocopier paper boxes (from your church office)
  - widemouth plastic containers

Organize Teaching Resources

Clearly label all items and cover recycled containers with contact plastic, if desired. Sections of a preschool resource room should include:

1. Art materials (paint supplies, smocks, easel, chalk, construction paper, butcher paper, sponges, cotton swabs, craft sticks, chenille craft stems, yarn, collage materials, and items for gadget and marble painting);
2. Books (from leader packs as well as other appropriate books, filed by concept or subject matter);
3. Block accessories (stand-up figures of people and animals, transportation toys, Legos®, Lincoln Logs®, boxes, other building materials);
4. Homeliving items (modern and Bible-times dress-up clothing, cleaning supplies, toy doctor's kit, doll, diaper bag and baby items, and plastic dishpans);
5. Musical instruments (Autoharp, step bells, and rhythm instruments);
6. Puzzles and manipulatives (recommended wooden and floor puzzles, parquet design blocks, lacing cards);
7. Nature items (pinecones, seashells, rocks, cotton boll, bird's nest, seed, feathers. magnets, magnifying glass);
8. Toys for babies and ones (balls, nesting toys, push-and-pull toys); and
9. Special equipment (sand/water table, toaster oven, electric skillet).

Discover New Uses for Household Discards

Collect and store these items for Bible learning activities and teacher-made toys.

- aluminum baking pans (various sizes)
- berry baskets
- fabric and felt scraps
- film canisters with lids
- cardboard paper towel tubes
- gift wrap scraps (no cartoon or fantasy characters)
- grocery sacks (paper)
- juice cans with metal lids
- magazines and catalogs
- margarine tubs with lids
- plastic soft drink bottles
- ribbon and lace
- spray bottles
- thread spools
- cardboard canisters with lids (empty oatmeal boxes)
- Christmas cards, other greeting cards (with appropriate themes; no fantasy or cartoon designs)

NOTE: Food containers should be cleaned thoroughly before use. Do not store foam packing pieces as they are highly flammable. Do not attempt to reuse foam meat trays; they often contain bacteria that cannot be removed. Evaluate all donated items for safety.

Design a System for Filing Resources
- File large teaching resources in an empty photocopy paper boxes. Create dividers by subject areas (Old Testament, New Testament, Jesus—birth and childhood, Jesus—ministry, Present-Day Pictures).
- Smaller teaching pictures can be stored in vinyl sheet protectors in a three-ring binder. Divide the pictures by subject areas (see list above).
- Games and the instructions for using them can be stored in zip-lock bags, pocket file folders (or regular file folders stapled on each side), or manila envelopes. Label each game according to the concept area.
- Create other dividers for filing items such as block accessories, music, recipes, instructions and patterns for teacher-made resources, or administrative and outreach items.
- Store books in pocket file folders or a detergent box covered with contact plastic. File by subject or concept.
- Bible markers may be sorted by references, placed in envelopes, and stored in a sturdy shoe box.

Setting Up a Resource Notebook
- Articles from leader's guides, conference handouts, and other resources can be placed in a preschool ministry notebook. Locate a three-ring binder, and use dividers to create sections such as: administration; Bible-learning centers/activities (art, homeliving, puzzles, blocks, music, books, and nature); ministry and outreach; health, safety, and security; or policies and legal issues.

Don't Despair if You Have "Too Many" Resources
If your church has an abundance of games, books, and Bible markers use them as outreach tools.
- Books, games, Bible markers, and learner's guides, can be given away during home or hospital visits.
- Some of these items, can be placed in "quiet activity sacks" that preschoolers can take into worship service.
- Books with your church's name and address can be placed, with permission, in a pediatrician's waiting room.
- Mission churches or shelters in your area also may be able to utilize such resources.

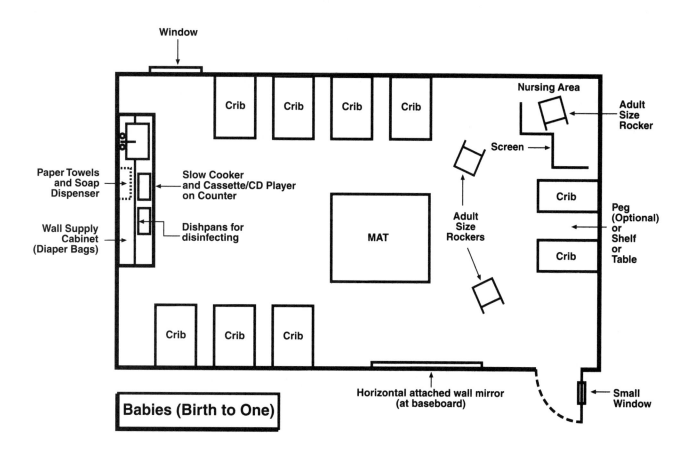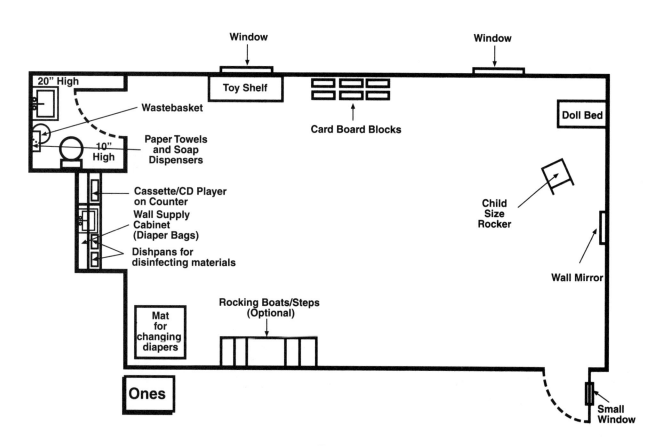

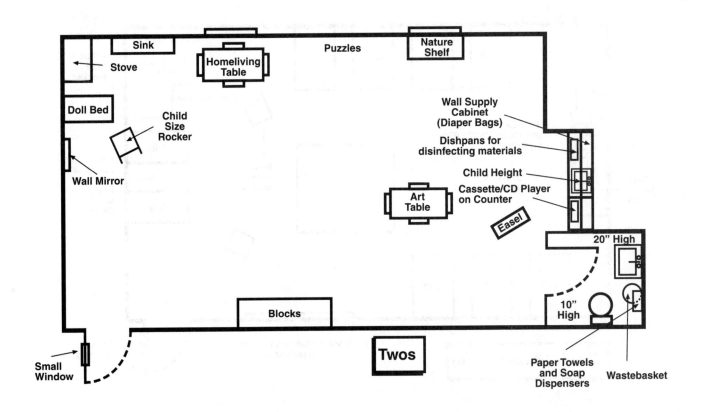
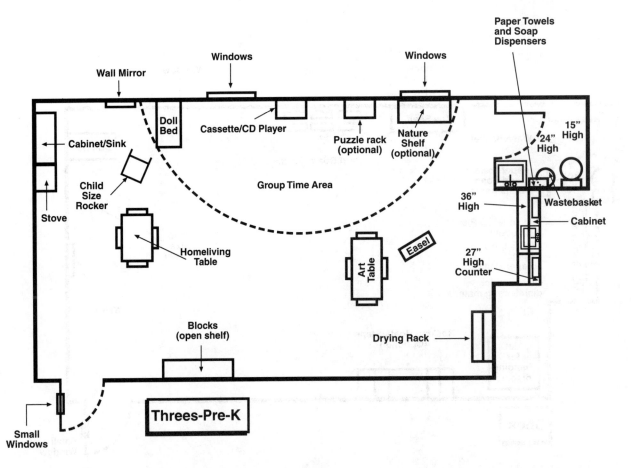

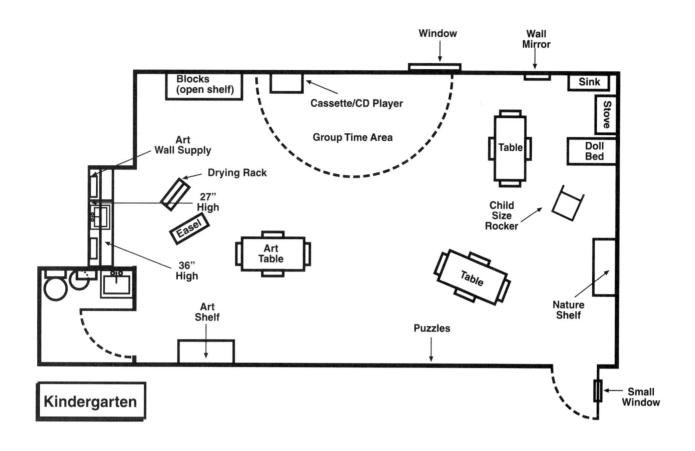

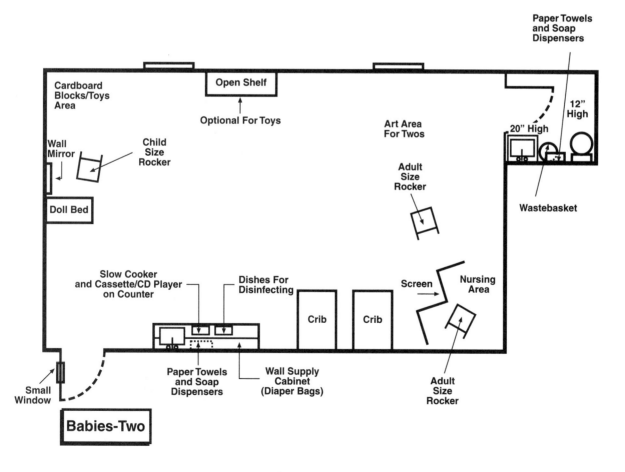

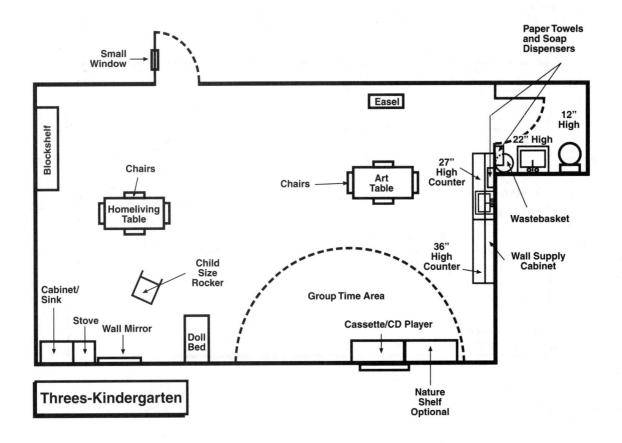
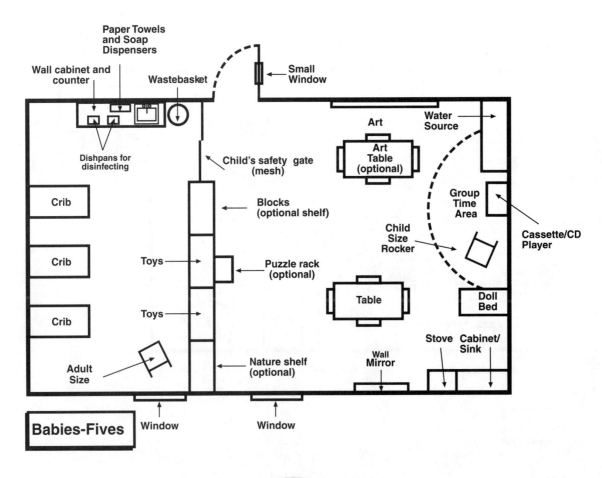

Studying This Book

Use this two-and-one-half-hour conference outline as a guide to plan a group study of *Preschool Sunday School for a New Century*. You can lead preschool leaders in an all-day study or several shorter training sessions. Consider using one or two teaching activities during leadership planning meetings over the course of a few months. However you choose to study this book, plan to review its contents so that your church can reach preschool families and teach preschoolers more effectively as you move into the new century.

Getting Ready:

- Arrange chairs in a semi-circle. Place an adhesive nametag in each chair.
- Arrange a *Read to Me Bible for Kids*; *Preschool Sunday School for a New Century*; *Just Like Jesus*; *Love, Laughter, and Learning*; and *Good News for Preschoolers and Their Families* on a table Scatter Kiddy Links® or other linking, chain-type toys and a Rock-a-Stack among the display items.
- Print each of the following Kent and Maria stories on separate sheets of paper: chapter 1 page 6; chapter 2 page 12; chapter 3 page 22; chapter 4 page 36; chapter 5 page 46; chapter 6 page 56 and page 66 (Maria). Number the stories one through seven. Enlist two conferees to read the stories throughout the conference.
- On the focal wall, tape two or three pictures of preschoolers (various ages). Leave an open space and then tape pictures of the Bible and Jesus on the wall.
- Cut paper into oval shapes to resemble chain links. Print these words on the links, one phrase per link: *Sunday School*, *preschoolers*, *leadership*, *organization*, *learning environment*, *ministry*, and *Bible teaching*.
- Print these questions on large pieces of paper, one statement per sheet: "Sunday School is. . ."; "Preschoolers are. . ."; "The 21st century is. . .". Tape the sheets to the walls around the room. Place markers near each sheet.
- Print Deuteronomy 6:5-7 on an index card and place in a Bible. Give Bible to a conferee.
- Write each of the Strategic Principles on paper strips (pp. 9-10) with the appropriate icon attached. Place the strips under chairs. Print the principles for preschool Sunday School (pp. 10-11) on a large piece of paper.
- Prepare an index card with scrambled letters of each of the needs of preschoolers (pp. 12-13).
- Cut a child shape from poster board. Cut the shape into eight pieces. Print preschool characteristics on the pieces.
- Make copies of the sample grouping/grading chart in chapter 3.
- Print the characteristics of a preschool teacher on paper strips.
- Prepare these group assignments. Place each assignment in a gift bag. Include materials needed to complete the assignment.
  Group 1: Discuss where to locate potential preschool teachers and the enlistment process. See chapter 4 for more information. Prepare a skit illustrating an enlisting visit.
  Group 2: Discuss the different types of training for preschool teachers. See chapter 4 for more information. Plan a one-hour training event. Decide on topic, theme, and other details. Make a poster advertising the event.
  Group 3: Discuss ways to show appreciation to preschool teachers. See chapter 4 for more information. Write an article or short blurb for a church newsletter to thank preschool teachers.
- Prepare these case studies on paper. Mount the paper on construction paper.
  1. Jonathan and Debbie are new parents. They are excited but unsure. They do not attend church anywhere.
  2. Hiroshi's company transferred him to your town. His family enjoyed their church at home. His wife Emiko and son Toshio speak little English. They are having difficulty adjusting to a new home and a new country.
  3. Two-year-old Kenisha is hearing impaired. She and her family visited your church and she had fun in Sunday School. Her parents wonder if your church can help Kenisha learn about God.
  4. Stephen and Alisha are nervous. "Bailey begins attending worship next month," Alisha says. "What are we going to do?"
- Print the ways preschoolers learn and the descriptions on index cards, one per card. Duplicate the *Making the Connection* on

page 61.
- Print the name of each learning center on a large sheet of paper (one per sheet). Leave space under title to write.

Leading the Session:

1. As conferees arrive, ask them to make nametags and write comments on each sheet to complete the statements.
2. Ask readers to read story number one. Say, "Like Maria and Kent, we will be looking at how our church will reach families in the future." Review comments related to the 21st Century. Say: "The 21st Century is an exciting time. It is also an uncertain time but the future is always uncertain. Preschoolers and their families need to know about God, the certainty in an uncertain future. In fact, God tells us to guide children toward Him."
3. Ask a conferee to read Deuteronomy 6:5-7. After the verse is read, discuss what the passage says about guiding children toward God. Pray, thanking God for the opportunities to teach about Him.
4. Say: "The Bible is our connection to God. It contains His words for us and is the foundation of all we do. We as preschool teachers want to connect preschoolers to the Bible. Today, we will discuss some ways we can help preschoolers connect with the Bible and Jesus." Point to the pictures of the Bible and Jesus and the preschoolers.
5. Say: "Sunday School is a very important link in connecting preschoolers to God through the Bible." Attach the *Sunday School* link on the wall by of the Bible. (You will build a chain from the Bible to the preschoolers with other links.) Read the comments on the sheet related to Sunday School. Then read the definition of Sunday School (p. 8). Discuss how this definition of Sunday School relates to preschool Sunday School (p. 10).
6. Tell conferees to look under their chairs and remove the paper strips with the principles of Sunday School. Read the principles, one at a time. Tape the principles to the focal wall, discussing each principle as you post it. Draw attention to preschool Sunday School principles and discuss how they relate to each other.
7. Read story two. Review comments about preschoolers on the sheet. Say, "Understanding preschoolers is another vital link in connecting preschoolers to the Bible." Attach the *Preschoolers* link on the wall. Continue, "Preschoolers are all different, but they have common needs and common characteristics."
8. Divide the group into twos and threes. Give each small group a *need* card. Tell the groups to unscramble the words on the cards and discuss how teachers can meet those needs. (Look in chapter 2 for more information.) After a few minutes, listen to the group reports. Fill in any necessary information.
9. Attach one piece at a time of the characteristics puzzle on the wall. Invite conferees to comment on each characteristic. Add other comments as necessary. Ask conferees to gather into groups by the ages they teach: babies, ones, twos, threes, fours/Pre-K, and kindergarten. Ask each group to make a list of the characteristics of their age group. The groups can compare their lists to the lists in chapter 2. Encourage groups to discuss how characteristics impact teaching.
10. Discuss how teachers can influence the spiritual development of preschoolers. "Who is the child's first and most significant teacher?" Comment that parents are the primary spiritual teachers in the preschoolers' lives and that we serve as partners with them.
11. Read story three. Add the *organization* link to the focal wall. Say, "Organizing the preschool ministry is essential to providing strong connections to the Bible." Discuss options for grouping preschoolers. Review teacher/child ratios. Give each conferee a copy of the sample grouping/grading chart and practice using it to determine where a child would be located. Call attention to the blank chart in the appendix. Discuss other organizational issues—creating new classes/departments, multiple Sunday Schools, sharing space.
12. Divide into three small groups. Give each group one of these questions to discuss: "What is ETC?" "Why develop policies and procedures?"; "Why are leadership meetings important?" Refer the groups to chapter 3. After a few minutes, call for group reports.
13. As you place the *learning environment* link on the focal wall, say, "Because the learning environment creates an atmosphere for learning Bible truths, it is an important link for connecting preschoolers to the Bible."
14. Divide by age groups again. Each group can look at the equipment list and room arrangement charts for their age groups. Encourage

conferees to discuss what are "musts" for a room and what are more flexible items.

15. Discuss factors that contribute to a positive learning environment for preschoolers. Read the guidelines on what to sacrifice, if necessary, in creating a learning environment for preschoolers (pp. 66-67).

16. Read story four. Place the *leadership* link on the wall. Say, "Providing committed preschool leaders is a strong link in connecting to the Bible." Give each conferee a piece of paper. Say, "List as many characteristics of a preschool teacher as you can in 10 seconds. Go!" After 10 seconds, say, "Stop!"

17. Place strips with the teacher characteristics on the wall, one at a time as you discuss each one. Encourage conferees to check characteristics off their lists that match the strips. Discuss all the strips; talk about the characteristics that conferees on their lists.

18. Divide into three small groups. Give each an assignment. After a few minutes, call for group reports on enlisting teachers, training teachers, and appreciating teachers. Call attention to the list of responsibilities of preschool leaders in chapter 4.

19. Read story five. Discuss the first paragraph in chapter 5 (after the scenario). Say, "Preschool teachers are ministers." Attach the *ministry* link.

20. Distribute the case studies. After the case study is read, lead a discussion on how to minister to the family. (Use information in chapter 5 as a guide.) As appropriate, include information on FIRST CONTACT, ministering to families from other cultures, ministering to children with special needs, contact 1-2-3, FAITH, and getting ready for worship.

21. Read story six. Ask conferees to respond to the question, "How are they going to learn about the Bible if they are playing?" Place the *Bible teaching* link on the focal wall.

22. Distribute the ways preschoolers learn. Read the cards. Discuss how preschoolers learn and how that impacts teaching.

23. Discuss the approaches to learning. Give the conferees a copy of the "Making the Connection" handout. Ask conferees to work with a partner. Review answers.

24. Post the learning center sheets. Ask conferees to list items/materials used in each center. After a few minutes, discuss each center and how it addresses the ways preschoolers learn and learning approaches.

25. Read story seven. Say: "God commands us to teach preschoolers about Him. As preschool teachers, we have the privilege and responsibility to help preschoolers connect with the Bible. What a wonderful opportunity we have to impact the 21st Century!" Pray.

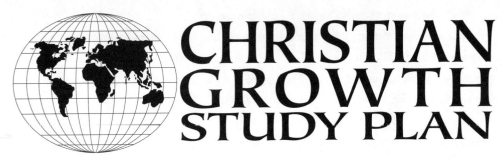

Preparing Christians to Serve

In the **Christian Growth Study Plan (formerly Church Study Course)**, this book *Preschool Sunday School for a New Century* is a resource for course credit in two Leadership and Skill Development diploma plans. To receive credit, read the book, complete the learning activities, show your work to your pastor, a staff member or church leader, then complete the following information. This page may be duplicated. Send the completed page to:

**Christian Growth Study Plan
127 Ninth Avenue, North
Nashville, TN 37234-0117
FAX: (615)251-5067**

For information about the Christian Growth Study Plan, refer to the current Christian Growth Study Plan Catalog. Your church office may have a copy. If not, request a free copy from the Christian Growth Study Plan office (615/251-2525).

COURSE CREDIT INFORMATION

Please check the appropriate box indicating the course(s) you want to apply this credit. You may check more than one.

- ❏ **The Administration of Preschool Ministries** (LS-0013, Sunday School)

- ❏ **Leadership Development of the Associational Leader** (LS-0068, Sunday School)

PARTICIPANT INFORMATION

Social Security Number (USA Only) | Personal CGSP Number* | Date of Birth (Mo., Day, Yr.)

Name (First, MI, Last) | Home Phone

Address (Street, Route, or P.O. Box) | City, State, or Province | Zip/Postal Code

CHURCH INFORMATION

Church Name

Address (Street, Route, or P.O. Box) | City, State, or Province | Zip/Postal Code

CHANGE REQUEST ONLY

Former Name

Former Address | City, State, or Province | Zip/Postal Code

Former Church | City, State, or Province | Zip/Postal Code

Signature of Pastor, Conference Leader, or Other Church Leader | Date

*New participants are requested but not required to give SS# and date of birth. Existing participants, please give CGSP# when using SS# for the first time. Thereafter, only one ID# is required. Mail To: Christian Growth Study Plan, 127 Ninth Avenue, North, Nashville, TN 37234-0117. Fax: (615)251-5067